Cascade Diplomacy

Managing Multi Crisis Politics in Unstable Times

Nelson Estrada

Chapter 1: Understanding Cascade Diplomacy

Defining Cascade Diplomacy in Modern Politics

The interconnected nature of modern global politics has given rise to a complex phenomenon where diplomatic challenges rarely exist in isolation. Cascade diplomacy emerges as a critical concept describing how political events, crises, and diplomatic interactions trigger chain reactions across international systems, creating multifaceted challenges that demand sophisticated responses from world leaders and diplomatic institutions.

At its core, cascade diplomacy represents the ripple effects of diplomatic actions and reactions that flow across borders, institutions, and political spheres. Unlike traditional diplomatic approaches that often address challenges in bilateral or isolated contexts, cascade diplomacy acknowledges the inherent interconnectedness of modern international relations and the potential for diplomatic actions to generate unexpected consequences across multiple domains.

The concept draws inspiration from various disciplines, including systems theory and network analysis, recognizing that modern diplomatic challenges operate within complex adaptive systems. When a significant diplomatic event occurs in one region, its effects can rapidly cascade through international networks, affecting trade relationships, security alliances, and cultural exchanges far beyond the initial point of impact.

Consider how economic sanctions against one nation can trigger retaliatory measures, affecting global supply chains, international trade agreements, and diplomatic relationships across multiple continents. These cascading effects often require diplomatic interventions at various levels, from bilateral negotiations to multilateral forums, creating a complex web of diplomatic engagement that characterizes modern international relations.

The digital revolution has amplified the cascade effect in diplomatic relations. Social media, instant global communications, and interconnected financial systems mean that diplomatic actions can have immediate and far-reaching consequences. A diplomatic statement made in one capital can instantly influence public opinion, market behavior, and political responses worldwide, requiring diplomats to navigate an increasingly complex and rapid-response environment.

Modern cascade diplomacy operates through various channels simultaneously. Traditional government-to-government interactions now occur alongside engagement with non-state actors, civil society organizations, multinational corporations, and international institutions. This multilayered approach reflects the reality that diplomatic challenges in the 21st century require coordinated responses across different sectors and stakeholders.

The concept also encompasses the way diplomatic crises can transform and evolve as they move across different contexts. An initial political dispute might evolve into an economic challenge, then trigger social unrest, and ultimately present security concerns, requiring diplomatic practitioners to possess diverse expertise and maintain flexibility in their approach.

Understanding cascade diplomacy requires recognition of both vertical and horizontal relationships in international relations. Vertical relationships include the interactions between local, national, and international levels of governance, while horizontal relationships span geographical regions and different policy domains. Successful diplomatic engagement often requires managing both dimensions simultaneously.

The practice of cascade diplomacy demands new skills and approaches from diplomatic practitioners. Traditional diplomatic training focused on bilateral relationships and protocol must now incorporate understanding of complex systems, network analysis, and rapid crisis response. Diplomats must develop the ability to anticipate how their actions might trigger cascading effects and prepare appropriate response strategies.

Risk assessment takes on new importance in cascade diplomacy. Diplomatic actors must evaluate not only the immediate consequences of their actions but also potential secondary and tertiary effects that might emerge across different domains and timeframes. This requires sophisticated modeling and scenario planning capabilities, along with deep understanding of regional and global interconnections.

The effectiveness of cascade diplomacy often depends on the strength of international institutions and frameworks that can help manage complex challenges. Regional organizations, international bodies, and informal diplomatic networks all play crucial roles in coordinating responses to cascading crises and maintaining stability in the international system.

Successful cascade diplomacy requires building resilient diplomatic relationships that can withstand stress and adapt to changing circumstances. This involves developing trust between parties, establishing clear communication channels, and creating flexible response mechanisms that can address emerging challenges before they escalate into larger crises.

Looking ahead, the importance of cascade diplomacy will likely continue to grow as global interconnections deepen and new challenges emerge. Climate change, technological disruption, and demographic shifts present complex challenges that will require sophisticated diplomatic approaches capable of managing multiple cascading effects across different domains and regions.

The concept of cascade diplomacy thus represents both a description of modern diplomatic reality and a framework for developing more effective diplomatic responses to complex global challenges. By understanding and embracing this approach, diplomatic practitioners can better navigate the interconnected challenges of the modern world and work toward more effective international cooperation and stability.

Historical Evolution of Multi Crisis Management

The practice of managing multiple simultaneous crises has evolved dramatically throughout human history, from ancient civilizations to our contemporary global society. Early instances of multi-crisis management can be traced to the Roman Empire, where leaders faced concurrent challenges of military invasions, internal political upheavals, and economic instabilities. The Romans developed sophisticated administrative systems and communication networks to handle these overlapping challenges, establishing precedents that would influence crisis management for centuries to come.

Medieval Europe witnessed the emergence of more structured approaches to crisis management, particularly during the period of the Black Death. Cities and states had to simultaneously address public health emergencies, maintain economic stability, and manage social order. Venice's response to multiple plague outbreaks exemplified early systematic crisis management, implementing quarantine measures while maintaining vital trade routes and diplomatic relations.

The Industrial Revolution marked a significant shift in crisis management complexity. The interconnected nature of industrial societies meant that local problems could quickly escalate into regional or national emergencies. The Great London Smog of 1952 demonstrated how environmental, public health, and governmental crises could intertwine, forcing authorities to develop more comprehensive response mechanisms.

The 20th century brought unprecedented challenges to crisis management systems. World War I represented a watershed moment, requiring nations to coordinate military operations while managing domestic economic pressures, diplomatic relations, and civilian needs. The interwar period saw the establishment of the League of Nations, marking the first attempt at creating an international framework for crisis prevention and management.

The Cold War era introduced new dimensions to multi-crisis management. The Cuban Missile Crisis of 1962 demonstrated how diplomatic, military, and communication crises could converge at a global scale. This period saw the development of sophisticated crisis response protocols and the establishment of dedicated crisis management centers in many nations.

The 1970s energy crisis revealed the intricate connections between resource management, economic stability, and international relations. Nations had to simultaneously address fuel shortages, inflation, and diplomatic tensions, leading to the creation of international energy coordination mechanisms and strategic petroleum reserves.

The late 20th century witnessed the emergence of more sophisticated crisis management frameworks. The United Nations Disaster Assessment and Coordination system, established in 1993, represented a major step forward in international crisis response coordination. Similar developments occurred in regional organizations, with the European Union creating various crisis response mechanisms.

The turn of the millennium brought new challenges to crisis management systems. The September 11 attacks in 2001 demonstrated how security, economic, and diplomatic crises could cascade globally within hours. This led to fundamental changes in how nations approach crisis preparation and response, including the creation of integrated command centers and enhanced international cooperation protocols.

Natural disasters like the 2004 Indian Ocean tsunami and Hurricane Katrina in 2005 revealed both the strengths and weaknesses of existing crisis management systems. These events highlighted the need for better coordination between different levels of government, improved communication systems, and more effective resource allocation mechanisms.

The evolution of technology has dramatically transformed crisis management capabilities. Satellite communications, data analytics, and real-time monitoring systems have enhanced the ability to track and respond to multiple crises simultaneously. However, these technological advances have also introduced new vulnerabilities and complexities to crisis management.

Financial crises have played a crucial role in shaping modern multi-crisis management approaches. The Asian Financial Crisis of 1997 and the Global Financial Crisis of 2008 led to the development of more robust international financial coordination mechanisms and early warning systems.

Recent decades have seen the emergence of more integrated approaches to crisis management. The concept of resilience has become central, focusing on building systems that can withstand multiple simultaneous shocks while maintaining essential functions. This has led to the development of more holistic crisis management frameworks that consider social, economic, and environmental factors.

The historical evolution of multi-crisis management reflects a growing understanding of the interconnected nature of global challenges. Each major crisis has contributed to the development of more sophisticated response mechanisms and coordination systems. This evolutionary process continues today, as nations and international organizations work to enhance their capacity to manage increasingly complex and interconnected crises.

Looking at this historical progression reveals key lessons about the importance of flexibility, coordination, and systemic thinking in crisis management. The most successful approaches have consistently been those that recognize the interconnected nature of crises and the need for coordinated, multi-level responses.

The Domino Effect in International Relations

Political events in the international arena rarely occur in isolation, instead following patterns reminiscent of falling dominoes, where one significant event triggers a sequence of related consequences across borders, regions, and continents. This interconnected nature of global politics creates complex chains of cause and effect that shape the modern diplomatic landscape.

The classic example of this phenomenon emerged during the Cold War era, when American foreign policy strategists developed the "domino theory" to describe how political changes in one country could rapidly spread to neighboring nations. While originally applied to the spread of communist influence in Southeast Asia, this conceptual framework has evolved to encompass a broader understanding of how political, economic, and social changes propagate across international boundaries.

Modern manifestations of the domino effect appear in various forms. The Arab Spring demonstrations of 2010-2012 powerfully illustrated how political upheaval in one nation could inspire similar movements across an entire region. Beginning with protests in Tunisia, the movement quickly spread to Egypt, Libya, Yemen, and Syria, demonstrating the contagious nature of political change in an interconnected world.

Economic domino effects have become increasingly prominent in our globalized economy. The Asian Financial Crisis of 1997 demonstrated how economic instability in Thailand could quickly spread across

Southeast Asia, affecting markets from Indonesia to South Korea. Similarly, the collapse of Lehman Brothers in 2008 triggered a chain reaction that reverberated through global financial markets, affecting economies worldwide.

Trade relationships create particularly vulnerable channels for domino effects. When major economies implement protectionist policies, the ripple effects can trigger retaliatory measures, leading to trade wars that affect multiple nations and sectors. These economic dominoes often spill over into diplomatic relations, creating complex challenges for international negotiators and policymakers.

Social movements and cultural trends also demonstrate domino-like patterns of transmission across borders. The global response to climate change illustrates how environmental awareness and policy initiatives can spread from one nation to another, creating momentum for international cooperation and action. Similarly, social justice movements often transcend national boundaries, inspiring parallel movements in different countries.

Technology and social media have accelerated the speed at which domino effects propagate in international relations. Information sharing occurs almost instantaneously, allowing political movements, economic trends, and social changes to spread more rapidly than ever before. This increased velocity of change presents new challenges for diplomatic practitioners and policymakers.

The refugee crisis in Europe demonstrated how humanitarian challenges can create cascading effects across multiple nations. The initial flow of refugees from Syria led to political tensions between European Union members, influenced domestic politics in numerous countries, and triggered changes in border policies across the continent. This complex chain of events continues to influence European politics and international relations.

Security relationships also exhibit domino-like patterns. Changes in military alliances or security arrangements often prompt responsive adjustments from other nations, creating chains of strategic repositioning. The expansion of military alliances or the development of new security partnerships frequently triggers responsive actions from potential adversaries, leading to complex security dynamics.

Regional organizations play a crucial role in managing and sometimes amplifying domino effects. The European Union's structure means that political decisions in one member state can have immediate implications for the entire bloc. Similarly, regional trade agreements create frameworks where economic changes in one country directly affect partners through established mechanisms.

Understanding these domino effects requires sophisticated analytical tools and frameworks. Traditional diplomatic approaches focused on bilateral relationships must be supplemented with network analysis and systems thinking to comprehend the complex ways in which international events influence each other.

Prevention and management of negative domino effects have become crucial diplomatic skills.

Successful diplomats must anticipate potential chain reactions and work to prevent or modify their progression. This requires deep understanding of regional dynamics, cultural contexts, and the complex interplay between different policy domains.

The role of international institutions in managing domino effects has grown increasingly important. Organizations like the United Nations, International Monetary Fund, and World Bank work to prevent negative cascading effects and promote positive ones through coordinated international action.

Looking ahead, the interconnected nature of international relations suggests that domino effects will continue to shape global politics. Climate change, technological innovation, and demographic shifts present challenges that will likely trigger complex chains of international responses and adjustments.

Understanding and managing these domino effects has become essential for effective international relations. Success in modern diplomacy requires the ability to anticipate potential chain reactions, develop preventive measures, and guide inevitable changes in constructive directions. This understanding forms a crucial foundation for effective international engagement in an increasingly interconnected world.

Theoretical Frameworks for Crisis Interconnectivity

Interconnected crises operate within complex theoretical frameworks that help explain their emergence, progression, and potential resolutions.

These frameworks draw from various disciplines, including systems theory, network analysis, chaos theory, and social dynamics, providing essential tools for understanding how multiple crises interact and influence each other across different domains.

Systems theory offers a fundamental basis for understanding crisis interconnectivity by emphasizing the relationships between different components within a larger system. When applied to crisis analysis, this approach reveals how disturbances in one part of a system can create ripple effects throughout the entire structure. For instance, environmental disasters often trigger economic disruptions, which in turn can lead to social unrest and political instability.

Network theory provides another crucial perspective by examining how connections between different actors and institutions influence crisis propagation. Through this lens, we can understand how information flows, resource distribution, and power relationships affect crisis development and management. The concept of network centrality helps identify key nodes where interventions might be most effective in preventing crisis escalation.

The butterfly effect, derived from chaos theory, explains how small changes in initial conditions can lead to significant consequences throughout interconnected systems. This principle is particularly relevant when analyzing how seemingly minor incidents can trigger major international crises through complex chains of cause and effect.

Social contagion theory offers insights into how crises can spread through populations and across borders. This framework helps explain phenomena such as financial panic, political unrest, and social movements that often characterize interconnected crises. Understanding these patterns of transmission is crucial for developing effective intervention strategies.

Complexity theory provides tools for analyzing how multiple variables interact in non-linear ways during crisis situations. This approach helps explain why traditional, linear problem-solving methods often fail when dealing with interconnected crises and why adaptive, flexible responses are necessary.

Game theory contributes valuable insights into strategic decision-making during crisis situations, particularly when multiple actors with competing interests are involved. This framework helps predict how different stakeholders might respond to crisis interventions and how their actions could affect overall system stability.

Resilience theory offers perspectives on how systems can maintain functionality despite multiple simultaneous pressures. This framework emphasizes the importance of redundancy, diversity, and adaptability in crisis management systems, helping to identify ways to build more robust response capabilities.

Path dependency theory explains how historical decisions and events constrain current options for crisis response. This framework is particularly useful for understanding why certain crisis management approaches may work in some contexts but fail in others, based on pre-existing institutional arrangements and cultural factors.

Organizational learning theory provides insights into how institutions can improve their crisis management capabilities through experience and adaptation. This framework emphasizes the importance of systematic analysis of past crises to develop more effective response mechanisms for future challenges.

The concept of nested systems helps explain how crises at different scales interact and influence each other. Local crises can escalate to national or international levels, while global crises can have distinct local manifestations requiring tailored responses at multiple levels simultaneously.

Feedback loop theory illuminates how crisis responses can either amplify or dampen system disturbances. Understanding these dynamics is crucial for developing interventions that prevent crisis escalation while promoting system stability.

Risk society theory, developed by sociologist Ulrich Beck, provides a framework for understanding how modern societies produce and distribute risks across different domains. This perspective helps explain why crises increasingly transcend traditional boundaries and require coordinated responses.

Cultural theory offers insights into how different societies perceive and respond to crises based on their values and beliefs. This framework is essential for developing culturally appropriate crisis management strategies in diverse international contexts.

Institutional theory helps explain how formal and informal rules shape crisis response capabilities and constraints. This perspective is particularly valuable for understanding why similar crises might produce different outcomes in different institutional contexts.

These theoretical frameworks, when integrated, provide a comprehensive foundation for understanding crisis interconnectivity. They help explain why crises rarely occur in isolation and why effective responses must account for multiple interacting factors across different domains.

The practical application of these frameworks requires careful consideration of context and scale. What works at one level may not be effective at another, and solutions must be adapted to specific circumstances while maintaining awareness of broader system dynamics.

Understanding these theoretical frameworks is essential for developing effective crisis management strategies. They provide the conceptual tools needed to analyze complex situations, anticipate potential developments, and design appropriate interventions that account for the interconnected nature of modern crises.

Key Players and Stakeholders in Cascade Diplomacy

Cascade diplomacy operates through a complex network of actors, each playing distinct yet interconnected roles in managing international crises and their ripple effects. At the highest level, national governments remain central figures, with heads of state and foreign ministers serving as primary decision-makers in diplomatic negotiations. Their actions and decisions create waves that influence multiple diplomatic channels simultaneously.

Diplomatic corps, including ambassadors and their staff, function as crucial intermediaries, maintaining communication channels and relationships even during periods of heightened tension. Their daily interactions and behind-the-scenes efforts often prevent minor disagreements from escalating into full-blown diplomatic crises.

International organizations, particularly the United Nations and its specialized agencies, serve as vital platforms for multilateral engagement. The UN Security Council, with its permanent and rotating members, plays a pivotal role in addressing interconnected security challenges. Similarly, the UN General Assembly provides a forum where smaller nations can voice concerns and participate in global decision-making processes.

Regional organizations have emerged as increasingly important players in cascade diplomacy. The European Union, African Union, and Association of Southeast Asian Nations (ASEAN) often serve as first responders to regional crises, coordinating responses among member states and managing diplomatic spillover effects.

Non-governmental organizations (NGOs) contribute significantly to cascade diplomacy through their expertise, networks, and ability to operate across borders. Organizations focused on humanitarian aid, environmental protection, and human rights often provide crucial information and facilitate unofficial diplomatic channels when formal ones become strained.

Financial institutions, including the World Bank and International Monetary Fund, wield considerable influence through their ability to provide economic support or impose conditions that affect multiple nations simultaneously. Their decisions can trigger cascading effects across global financial markets and international relations.

Multinational corporations have become influential stakeholders in cascade diplomacy, as their operations and decisions can significantly impact international relations. Corporate diplomacy often intersects with traditional diplomatic channels, particularly in areas such as trade disputes, technology transfer, and environmental regulations.

Think tanks and research institutions play a vital role by providing analysis and policy recommendations that shape diplomatic approaches. Their expertise helps stakeholders understand the complex interconnections between different aspects of international crises and potential solutions.

Media organizations, both traditional and digital, influence cascade diplomacy by shaping public opinion and affecting the speed at which diplomatic situations evolve. Their coverage can either amplify or mitigate tensions, making them crucial players in modern diplomatic processes.

Civil society organizations, including advocacy groups and professional associations, contribute to cascade diplomacy by mobilizing public support, sharing specialized knowledge, and maintaining unofficial channels of communication during crises.

Religious leaders and institutions often serve as unexpected but influential diplomatic actors, particularly in regions where religious and political affairs intersect. Their moral authority and transnational networks can help mediate conflicts and promote dialogue across cultural boundaries.

Academic institutions contribute through research, training future diplomats, and maintaining international educational exchanges that build long-term relationships between nations. Their expertise often provides crucial context for understanding complex diplomatic situations.

Local governments, particularly those of major cities, increasingly engage in paradiplomacy, forming international networks to address shared challenges like climate change and migration. Their actions can significantly influence national diplomatic positions and international cooperation.

Indigenous peoples' organizations have emerged as important voices in diplomatic discussions, particularly regarding environmental protection, cultural preservation, and resource management. Their perspectives often highlight overlooked aspects of international challenges.

Youth organizations and movements have gained prominence in cascade diplomacy, particularly regarding climate action and social justice. Their ability to mobilize across borders and use social media effectively makes them increasingly influential in shaping diplomatic agendas.

Professional diplomats must navigate this complex web of stakeholders while maintaining coherent diplomatic strategies. Success requires understanding how different actors' interests and capabilities interact, and how to leverage these relationships effectively during crises.

The effectiveness of cascade diplomacy often depends on the ability of these various stakeholders to coordinate their efforts and maintain clear communication channels. When multiple actors work at cross-purposes, diplomatic efforts can become confused and counterproductive.

Understanding the roles and relationships between these key players is essential for effective diplomatic practice in today's interconnected world. Each stakeholder brings unique capabilities and perspectives to diplomatic processes, and successful outcomes often depend on leveraging these diverse contributions effectively.

The challenge lies in orchestrating these various actors toward common objectives while respecting their different priorities and constraints. Modern diplomatic practice requires sophisticated stakeholder management skills and an appreciation for the complex ways in which different actors influence each other.

Chapter 2: The Architecture of Modern Crises

Mapping Crisis Networks and Dependencies

Crisis networks form intricate webs of relationships that connect various events, actors, and consequences across geographical and temporal boundaries. Understanding these complex interconnections requires sophisticated mapping techniques that reveal both obvious and subtle dependencies between different crisis elements.

Network mapping begins with identifying primary nodes - the key events, institutions, or conditions that serve as focal points in a crisis situation. These nodes might include financial institutions during economic crises, government agencies during political upheavals, or critical infrastructure during natural disasters. Each node represents a potential point of failure or intervention in the broader crisis network.

Dependencies between nodes manifest in various forms, from direct causal relationships to subtle feedback loops that may not become apparent until a crisis is well underway. For instance, the relationship between energy infrastructure and financial markets creates critical dependencies that can trigger cascading failures when disrupted. During the 2021 Texas power crisis, the failure of electrical systems led to disruptions in water treatment facilities, which in turn affected healthcare services, creating a complex chain of interconnected crises.

Temporal mapping reveals how crisis networks evolve over time, showing how initial disruptions can lead to secondary and tertiary effects that may not manifest immediately. This temporal dimension is crucial for understanding how crises develop and identifying potential intervention points before situations deteriorate further.

Geographic information systems (GIS) play a vital role in crisis network mapping, allowing analysts to visualize how crises spread across regions and borders. These tools help identify spatial patterns and relationships that might not be apparent from data alone. The spread of supply chain disruptions during the global pandemic demonstrated how geographic dependencies can amplify crisis effects across continents.

Resource flow mapping tracks the movement of critical supplies, information, and support through crisis networks. This approach helps identify bottlenecks and vulnerable points in supply chains, communication systems, and response networks. Understanding these flows is essential for maintaining critical services during crisis situations.

Social network analysis reveals how information, influence, and support move through human networks during crises. This methodology helps identify key influencers, communication channels, and community structures that can either mitigate or exacerbate crisis effects. The role of social media networks in spreading both accurate information and misinformation during crises exemplifies the importance of understanding these social connections.

Infrastructure dependency mapping shows how different systems rely on each other for normal operation. Power grids depend on communication networks, which in turn require electricity to function. Water systems need power for pumping and treatment, while transportation networks rely on multiple infrastructure systems to operate effectively. Understanding these interdependencies is crucial for preventing cascade failures.

Financial network mapping reveals the complex relationships between financial institutions, markets, and economic systems. These maps help predict how financial shocks can propagate through the global economy and identify potential stabilizing interventions. The 2008 financial crisis demonstrated the importance of understanding these intricate financial dependencies.

Organizational network analysis examines how different institutions and agencies interact during crisis situations. This approach helps identify gaps in coordination, overlapping responsibilities, and potential conflicts that could hamper crisis response efforts. Effective crisis management requires clear understanding of these organizational relationships.

Risk pathway mapping traces how various risks can combine and interact to create complex crisis scenarios. This technique helps identify potential trigger points and intervention opportunities before crises fully develop. Understanding risk pathways allows for more proactive crisis management approaches.

Cultural and social dependency mapping examines how different communities and social groups are interconnected during crises. This analysis helps predict how social tensions or cultural factors might influence crisis development and response effectiveness. Recognition of these social dependencies is crucial for developing culturally appropriate crisis interventions.

Technology dependency mapping reveals how different systems rely on specific technologies and how technological failures can cascade through multiple systems. As societies become more technologically integrated, understanding these dependencies becomes increasingly critical for crisis management.

Environmental system mapping shows how natural systems interact with human infrastructure and activities during crises. This approach helps predict how environmental changes might trigger or exacerbate other types of crises, from food security issues to population displacement.

Regulatory and policy dependency mapping examines how different rules, regulations, and policies interact during crises. This analysis helps identify potential conflicts or gaps in regulatory frameworks that could complicate crisis response efforts.

The integration of these various mapping approaches provides a comprehensive understanding of crisis networks and dependencies. This holistic view enables more effective crisis prediction, prevention, and response strategies. Modern crisis management requires sophisticated understanding of these complex networks and the ability to navigate their various interdependencies effectively.

Digital Age Amplification of Crisis Cascades

Digital technologies have fundamentally transformed how crises develop, spread, and impact societies across the globe. The interconnected nature of modern digital systems creates new pathways for crisis propagation while simultaneously offering novel tools for crisis management and response.

Social media platforms serve as powerful accelerants for crisis cascades, enabling information—and misinformation—to spread at unprecedented speeds. A single tweet or viral post can trigger stock market fluctuations, spark social unrest, or initiate diplomatic incidents within hours. During the 2020 global health crisis, social media simultaneously facilitated vital information sharing and accelerated the spread of harmful conspiracy theories, demonstrating the double-edged nature of digital amplification.

Financial markets have become particularly susceptible to digital cascade effects. High-frequency trading algorithms can react to news events in milliseconds, potentially triggering market-wide selloffs before human traders can intervene. The 2010 Flash Crash exemplified how digital systems can amplify market disruptions, causing a trillion-dollar market value drop within minutes.

Cybersecurity threats represent a unique form of crisis amplification in the digital age. A single security breach can rapidly cascade across interconnected networks, affecting multiple organizations and jurisdictions simultaneously. The 2017 WannaCry ransomware attack demonstrated how digital vulnerabilities could quickly paralyze essential services across continents.

Digital supply chain dependencies create new forms of crisis vulnerability. Modern businesses rely on complex networks of digital services and infrastructure, making them susceptible to cascading failures when key systems are compromised. Cloud computing outages can affect thousands of businesses simultaneously, creating widespread economic disruptions.

The Internet of Things (IoT) introduces additional layers of complexity to crisis cascades. Connected devices in critical infrastructure, healthcare, and transportation systems create new potential failure points that can trigger chain reactions across multiple sectors. A compromised industrial control system could potentially affect power distribution, water treatment, and manufacturing processes simultaneously.

Social polarization intensifies through digital echo chambers and algorithmic content recommendation systems. These technological features can accelerate the spread of extreme viewpoints and deepen societal divisions, making crisis management more challenging. Political crises now frequently feature digital components that complicate traditional resolution approaches.

Mobile technologies have transformed how people experience and respond to crises. While enabling rapid information sharing and emergency response coordination, mobile networks can also amplify panic and confusion during crisis situations. The constant flow of crisis-related information through personal devices can create psychological strain and decision paralysis.

Digital payment systems introduce new vulnerabilities to economic crises. The increasing reliance on electronic transactions means that technical failures or cyber attacks can quickly disrupt entire economies. The growing adoption of cryptocurrency adds another layer of complexity to financial crisis management.

Cloud infrastructure centralization creates potential single points of failure that could trigger widespread service disruptions. When major cloud providers experience outages, the effects ripple through countless dependent services and organizations, highlighting the risks of digital concentration.

Digital media ecosystems have transformed crisis communication dynamics. Traditional media gatekeepers have lost influence to social networks and online platforms, making it harder to maintain consistent crisis messaging. The rapid spread of deepfake videos and manipulated content adds new dimensions to crisis management challenges.

Smart city technologies, while offering improved efficiency and service delivery, create new pathways for crisis propagation. Interconnected urban systems can transmit disruptions across multiple services simultaneously, potentially affecting millions of residents in densely populated areas.

Digital surveillance capabilities introduce privacy and security concerns that can escalate into broader societal crises. The tension between security needs and privacy rights creates complex challenges for crisis management in the digital age.

Remote work infrastructure has become critical to organizational resilience, but also creates new vulnerabilities. The massive shift to remote operations during recent global crises highlighted both the benefits and risks of digital dependency in modern organizations.

Quantum computing developments may soon introduce new dimensions to digital crisis cascades. The potential to break current encryption methods could trigger widespread security crises across digital systems.

The acceleration of digital transformation across all sectors increases both the potential for and impact of crisis cascades. Organizations must balance the benefits of digital integration against the risks of increased vulnerability to cascading failures.

Crisis response strategies must evolve to address these digital age challenges. Traditional approaches often prove inadequate when dealing with the speed and complexity of digitally amplified crises. New frameworks must incorporate digital resilience and cyber-awareness at their core.

The future of crisis management lies in developing adaptive systems that can respond to rapidly evolving digital threats while maintaining essential services and social stability. Success requires understanding both the technical and human dimensions of digital crisis cascades.

Effective crisis management in the digital age demands new skills, tools, and approaches that account for the unique characteristics of digital amplification. Organizations and societies must build resilience while remaining flexible enough to adapt to emerging digital challenges.

Regional vs Global Crisis Dynamics

The interplay between regional and global crisis dynamics creates complex patterns of escalation and response that shape modern international relations. While regional crises may initially appear contained within specific geographical boundaries, they frequently transform into global challenges through various interconnection points and spillover effects.

Economic crises provide clear examples of how regional issues can rapidly acquire global dimensions. The 1997 Asian financial crisis began in Thailand but quickly spread throughout Southeast Asia before affecting markets worldwide. Similarly, the European debt crisis of 2009 started in Greece but threatened the stability of the entire Eurozone and, by extension, the global financial system.

Regional conflicts often draw in global powers through alliance systems, economic interests, and strategic considerations. The ongoing tensions in the South China Sea illustrate how territorial disputes between regional actors can evolve into broader geopolitical challenges involving major powers and international law. What begins as a regional maritime disagreement can escalate into a test of global security frameworks.

Environmental crises demonstrate particularly complex regional-global dynamics. Forest fires in the Amazon affect regional air quality and biodiversity while simultaneously impacting global carbon cycles and climate patterns. Regional environmental management decisions thus have direct global consequences, creating a need for coordinated response mechanisms that span multiple scales.

Supply chain disruptions highlight the intricate connections between regional and global crisis dynamics. A factory shutdown in one region can trigger production delays worldwide, as demonstrated by the semiconductor shortage that began in 2020. Regional infrastructure or labor issues can quickly cascade into global supply constraints.

Migration crises typically start as regional phenomena but frequently evolve into global challenges. The Syrian refugee crisis initially affected neighboring Middle Eastern countries but subsequently impacted European politics, international aid systems, and global humanitarian responses. Regional capacity limitations often necessitate broader international engagement.

Health emergencies reveal how quickly regional outbreaks can become global concerns. The SARS outbreak of 2003 began in southern China but rapidly spread internationally through air travel networks. Regional health system capabilities and response speeds can determine whether a local outbreak remains contained or becomes a global pandemic.

Cultural and social movements increasingly transcend regional boundaries through digital networks. Regional protests or social justice movements can quickly inspire global solidarity actions and policy responses. The interconnected nature of modern media ensures that regional social dynamics often acquire global significance.

Resource scarcity issues demonstrate complex regional-global feedback loops. Regional water shortages, for instance, can affect global food prices through agricultural impacts, while global climate change can exacerbate regional water stress. These interconnections require coordinated management approaches at multiple scales.

Political instability in key regions often has global ramifications through energy markets, trade routes, and security alliances. Regional political transitions can trigger international market reactions and strategic realignments that affect global stability. The interdependence of modern international systems means that regional political crises rarely remain purely local affairs.

Technology sector disruptions show how regional regulatory decisions can have global impacts. Regional data privacy laws, technology bans, or infrastructure decisions can affect global digital services and technology supply chains. The increasingly connected nature of digital systems means that regional technology policies often have global implications.

Natural disasters require careful coordination between regional and global response systems. While immediate impacts may be regional, effective response often requires global resources and expertise. The 2011 Tohoku earthquake and tsunami in Japan affected global supply chains and nuclear energy policies well beyond the immediate region.

Currency crises demonstrate how regional financial instability can threaten global economic systems. The collapse of regional currencies can trigger international market reactions and force policy responses from global financial institutions. Regional financial management decisions thus carry global implications.

Trade disputes between regional blocs can escalate into global economic challenges. Regional trade agreements and protectionist measures often have ripple effects throughout the global trading system, requiring careful management of both regional and global economic relationships.

Regional security arrangements increasingly interact with global security frameworks. NATO's activities in Europe, for example, have implications for global security dynamics and international military relationships. Regional security crises often require balancing local concerns with global strategic considerations.

Climate adaptation challenges reveal the necessity of coordinating regional and global responses. While climate impacts vary by region, effective adaptation requires both local action and global cooperation. Regional climate resilience efforts must align with global climate goals and support systems.

Understanding these complex dynamics requires sophisticated analytical frameworks that can track both regional and global crisis elements simultaneously. Success in modern crisis management depends on the ability to navigate these multiple scales effectively while maintaining coherence in response strategies.

The future of crisis management lies in developing flexible approaches that can address both regional specifics and global implications. Organizations and governments must build capabilities to operate effectively across these different scales while maintaining coordination between regional and global response mcchanisms.

Chapter 3: Strategic Response Mechanisms

Early Warning Systems and Prevention

Early warning systems serve as crucial frontline defenses against emerging crises, offering organizations and societies precious time to prepare and implement preventive measures. These systems combine technological capabilities, human expertise, and systematic monitoring to detect crisis signals before they develop into full-blown emergencies.

Effective early warning begins with comprehensive environmental scanning across multiple domains. Financial institutions monitor market indicators, currency fluctuations, and debt levels to identify potential economic crises. Environmental agencies track weather patterns, seismic activity, and pollution levels to predict natural disasters and ecological threats. Health organizations survey disease outbreaks and monitor antimicrobial resistance to prevent pandemic spread.

Signal detection requires sophisticated filtering mechanisms to distinguish meaningful indicators from background noise. Modern early warning systems employ advanced statistical models to identify anomalies and patterns that might indicate emerging threats. For instance, seismologists use networks of sensors to detect subtle ground movements that could presage major earthquakes, while epidemiologists track unusual disease patterns through healthcare data.

Social media monitoring has emerged as a vital component of contemporary early warning systems. By analyzing social media trends and sentiment, organizations can detect growing social tensions, political instability, or public health concerns before they become critical. During the Arab Spring, social media analysis provided early indicators of mounting political unrest.

Prevention strategies must be closely integrated with warning systems to be effective. When warning signs appear, organizations need clear protocols for escalating concerns and initiating preventive actions. The European Central Bank's financial stress testing system, for example, helps identify vulnerable banks and trigger preventive measures before financial crises develop.

Cross-border cooperation strengthens early warning capabilities significantly. International sharing of meteorological data improves tsunami warning systems, while global disease surveillance networks help contain potential pandemics. The World Health Organization's Global Outbreak Alert and Response Network exemplifies how international cooperation enhances early warning effectiveness.

Technological infrastructure plays a crucial role in modern warning systems. Satellite monitoring systems track environmental changes and potential natural disasters, while automated trading systems monitor financial markets for dangerous volatility. These technological capabilities must be balanced with human expertise to ensure accurate interpretation of warning signals.

Community engagement enhances early warning effectiveness substantially. Local communities often notice subtle changes in their environment that might escape automated monitoring systems. Indigenous knowledge of environmental patterns, combined with modern warning systems, provides more comprehensive threat detection capabilities.

Risk assessment frameworks help prioritize warning signals and allocate prevention resources efficiently. Organizations must evaluate potential threats based on both likelihood and impact, focusing preventive efforts where they will be most effective. Regular review and updating of risk assessments ensures warning systems remain relevant to evolving threats.

Communication protocols form a critical component of early warning systems. Clear, timely, and accurate communication of warnings to affected stakeholders can mean the difference between successful prevention and crisis escalation. Warning messages must be tailored to different audiences while maintaining consistency in core information.

Redundancy in warning systems provides crucial backup capabilities when primary systems fail. Multiple independent monitoring networks, diverse communication channels, and backup power systems ensure warning capabilities remain functional during emergencies. The Japanese earthquake warning system demonstrates how redundant systems enhance reliability.

Preventive maintenance of warning infrastructure ensures system reliability when needed most. Regular testing, updating, and repair of monitoring equipment and communication systems prevents failures during critical moments. Investment in system maintenance often proves far less costly than crisis response.

Training and simulation exercises help organizations maintain warning system effectiveness. Regular drills ensure staff understand warning protocols and can respond appropriately when real threats emerge. These exercises also help identify potential weaknesses in warning and prevention systems before actual crises occur.

Cultural factors significantly influence warning system effectiveness. Different societies respond to warnings in various ways, based on historical experience, trust in authorities, and cultural values. Effective warning systems must account for these cultural variations in their design and implementation.

Economic considerations often affect investment in warning systems and prevention measures. While the cost of implementing comprehensive warning systems may seem high, it typically pales in comparison to the cost of crisis response and recovery. The challenge lies in justifying preventive investments when threats remain theoretical.

Psychological factors influence how warnings are perceived and acted upon. Warning fatigue can develop when too many alerts are issued, while normalcy bias may cause people to underestimate serious threats. Understanding these psychological factors helps design more effective warning communications.

Legal frameworks provide essential support for warning systems and prevention measures. Clear legal mandates for warning issuance and response actions help overcome organizational inertia and ensure appropriate preventive actions are taken. These frameworks must balance the need for quick action with accountability requirements.

The future of early warning systems lies in integrating multiple data sources and analysis methods while maintaining human oversight and interpretation capabilities. Success requires continuous adaptation to emerging threats while preserving core warning and prevention capabilities. Organizations must remain committed to supporting and improving these critical systems despite competing priorities and resource constraints.

Multi stakeholder Coordination Protocols

Effective coordination among diverse stakeholders during crises requires carefully structured protocols that balance speed, accountability, and inclusive decision-making. These protocols establish clear lines of communication, define roles and responsibilities, and create frameworks for collaborative action across organizational boundaries.

Government agencies, private sector entities, non-governmental organizations, and community groups each bring unique capabilities and perspectives to crisis response efforts. The challenge lies in harmonizing these different approaches while maintaining operational efficiency. During the 2011 Fukushima disaster, coordination between nuclear plant operators, government regulators, and emergency response teams proved crucial for managing the complex crisis.

Clear hierarchical structures provide essential foundations for multi-stakeholder coordination. These structures must define decision-making authority while remaining flexible enough to accommodate different organizational cultures and capabilities. The Incident Command System used in emergency management demonstrates how hierarchical protocols can facilitate coordinated response while maintaining clear accountability.

Information sharing protocols form the backbone of effective coordination. Standardized reporting formats, regular briefing schedules, and secure communication channels ensure all stakeholders work from consistent information. During public health emergencies, protocols for sharing patient data between healthcare providers, public health agencies, and research institutions prove essential for coordinated response.

Resource allocation mechanisms require careful design to ensure fair and efficient distribution during crises. Protocols must balance immediate operational needs with longer-term strategic considerations while accounting for different stakeholder priorities. The Strategic National Stockpile system exemplifies how resource sharing protocols can support coordinated emergency response.

Cross-border coordination presents unique challenges that demand specialized protocols. Different legal systems, cultural norms, and operational standards must be reconciled to enable effective international cooperation. The European Union's Civil Protection Mechanism shows how formal protocols can facilitate coordinated response across national boundaries.

Technology platforms play crucial roles in supporting coordination protocols. Shared situational awareness tools, resource management systems, and communication platforms help stakeholders maintain coordination during complex operations. However, these systems must remain accessible and reliable under crisis conditions.

Financial protocols ensure smooth resource flows during crisis response operations. Clear procedures for emergency funding, cost sharing, and accountability help prevent delays in critical activities. The World Bank's Pandemic Emergency Financing Facility demonstrates how financial protocols can support rapid, coordinated response to global health crises.

Legal frameworks provide essential foundations for multi-stakeholder coordination. Memoranda of understanding, mutual aid agreements, and formal partnerships establish clear bases for cooperation while protecting stakeholder interests. These frameworks must balance the need for quick action with appropriate oversight and accountability.

Training and exercises help stakeholders familiarize themselves with coordination protocols before crises occur. Regular joint exercises identify potential coordination challenges and build relationships between stakeholder organizations. These activities prove particularly valuable when stakeholders must work together under pressure.

Cultural sensitivity remains essential for effective coordination across different organizations and communities. Protocols must accommodate various communication styles, decision-making processes, and organizational cultures while maintaining operational effectiveness. Success often depends on finding common ground while respecting differences.

Quality assurance mechanisms ensure coordination protocols remain effective over time. Regular review and updating of procedures, performance monitoring, and after-action assessments help identify and address coordination challenges. These mechanisms must balance the need for improvement with stability in core procedures.

Dispute resolution procedures help maintain coordination when conflicts arise between stakeholders. Clear protocols for addressing disagreements prevent operational disruptions while preserving important relationships. These procedures must be fair, transparent, and efficient to maintain stakeholder confidence.

Documentation requirements support accountability while facilitating learning from experience. Standardized recording procedures, decision logs, and after-action reports help organizations improve coordination over time. However, documentation demands must not impede operational effectiveness during crises.

Stakeholder engagement protocols ensure appropriate involvement of all relevant parties in coordination activities. Regular consultation mechanisms, feedback channels, and participation frameworks help maintain inclusive decision-making while preserving operational efficiency. These protocols must balance the need for broad participation with timely action.

Succession planning ensures coordination continues when key personnel change. Clear procedures for transferring responsibilities and maintaining institutional knowledge help preserve coordination capabilities over time. These protocols become particularly important during extended crisis responses.

Technology transition protocols help stakeholders adapt to new coordination tools and systems. Clear procedures for testing, implementing, and training on new technologies ensure coordinated operations continue smoothly during system changes. These protocols must balance innovation with operational stability.

The future of multi-stakeholder coordination lies in developing more adaptive and inclusive protocols while maintaining operational effectiveness. Success requires continuous refinement of coordination mechanisms based on experience while preserving core capabilities that support effective crisis response. Organizations must remain committed to strengthening coordination protocols despite the challenges of working across institutional boundaries.

Resource Allocation in Multiple Crisis Scenarios

Resource allocation during multiple simultaneous crises presents unique challenges that test the limits of emergency management systems and organizational capabilities. When multiple disasters or emergencies compete for limited resources, decision-makers must navigate complex trade-offs while maintaining effective response capabilities across all affected areas.

Strategic prioritization becomes essential when facing concurrent crises. During the 2017 hurricane season, emergency managers had to balance resources between multiple affected regions as successive storms struck different areas. This required careful assessment of immediate needs, available capabilities, and potential future developments to optimize resource distribution.

Personnel management presents particular challenges during multiple crisis scenarios. Skilled emergency responders, medical professionals, and technical experts often find themselves stretched thin across different emergency sites. The COVID-19 pandemic demonstrated how healthcare workers had to be strategically deployed across multiple hotspots while maintaining essential services elsewhere.

Equipment and supplies require careful allocation when multiple crises compete for resources.

Organizations must develop sophisticated logistics systems that can track, distribute, and redistribute critical supplies as needs evolve. The global supply chain disruptions of recent years have highlighted the importance of flexible resource allocation systems.

Financial resources demand strategic management during multiple crises. Emergency funds must be allocated across different response efforts while maintaining reserves for potential escalation or new emergencies. International aid organizations regularly face these challenges when responding to simultaneous humanitarian crises in different regions.

Transportation assets become critical resources during multiple crisis scenarios. Aircraft, vehicles, and vessels must be allocated efficiently between different emergency zones while maintaining essential services. Military organizations often demonstrate effective practices in managing transportation resources across multiple operational theaters.

Communication infrastructure requires careful allocation when multiple crises strain available bandwidth and equipment. Emergency communication systems must be distributed to support different response efforts while maintaining overall coordination capabilities. Satellite communication resources, in particular, often require strategic allocation during large-scale emergencies.

Expert knowledge represents a crucial resource that must be carefully managed during multiple crises. Technical specialists, crisis managers, and subject matter experts must be deployed where their expertise will have the greatest impact. Virtual consultation systems can help extend expert resources across multiple crisis locations.

Storage and staging facilities become vital resources when managing multiple crisis responses. Organizations must balance the need for forward-positioned supplies with maintaining strategic reserves for other potential emergencies. The Strategic National Stockpile system demonstrates how storage resources can be managed across multiple emergencies.

Time management takes on critical importance when handling multiple crises. Leaders must allocate their attention and decision-making capacity efficiently across different emergency situations while maintaining strategic oversight. Clear delegation protocols help organizations manage time resources effectively during complex scenarios.

Energy resources require strategic allocation during multiple crisis scenarios. Power generation and fuel supplies must be distributed to support different response efforts while maintaining essential services. The Texas power crisis of 2021 illustrated the challenges of managing energy resources across multiple emergency situations.

Information systems represent crucial resources that must be allocated effectively during multiple crises. Data processing capacity, analytical capabilities, and reporting systems must support different response efforts while maintaining overall situational awareness. Modern emergency operations centers demonstrate how information resources can be managed across multiple incidents.

Medical resources demand particularly careful allocation during multiple health emergencies. Hospital beds, medical equipment, and pharmaceutical supplies must be distributed based on careful assessment of needs and potential developments across different locations. The COVID-19 pandemic provided numerous lessons in medical resource allocation during complex crises.

Food and water supplies require strategic management when multiple crises affect different populations. Distribution systems must be optimized to support various emergency zones while maintaining essential services elsewhere. Humanitarian organizations regularly face these challenges when responding to multiple disasters.

Technological resources must be allocated effectively across different crisis responses. Monitoring equipment, communication devices, and specialized tools must be distributed based on operational priorities and technical requirements. Space-based assets often require particularly careful allocation during multiple emergencies.

Recovery resources demand strategic allocation even as response efforts continue. Organizations must balance immediate emergency needs with longer-term recovery requirements across different affected areas. This often requires difficult trade-offs between competing priorities and needs.

The future of resource allocation in multiple crisis scenarios lies in developing more sophisticated decision support systems while maintaining operational flexibility. Success requires careful balance between immediate tactical needs and strategic considerations across different emergency situations. Organizations must continue improving their capabilities to manage resources effectively across multiple concurrent crises.

Success in managing multiple crisis scenarios ultimately depends on building robust resource allocation systems before emergencies occur. These systems must combine clear protocols with flexibility to adapt to changing circumstances while maintaining effective support across different emergency situations. Regular testing and refinement of resource allocation capabilities helps organizations prepare for complex crisis scenarios.

Communication Strategies During Overlapping Crises

Communication strategies take on heightened importance when multiple crises intersect, demanding clear, consistent, and coordinated messaging across different emergency situations. The complexity of managing information flow during overlapping crises requires sophisticated approaches that balance transparency with accuracy while maintaining public trust.

Effective crisis communication begins with establishing clear authority structures for message approval and dissemination. During the 2008 financial crisis coinciding with natural disasters, organizations needed to coordinate messages about economic stability while addressing immediate safety concerns. This required careful orchestration between different communication teams and spokesperson networks.

Message prioritization becomes crucial when dealing with multiple emergencies. Communications teams must determine which information takes precedence while ensuring all critical messages reach their intended audiences. The challenge lies in preventing message fatigue while maintaining awareness of multiple threats. During the 2020 hurricane season amid public health concerns, emergency managers had to balance evacuation orders with pandemic safety guidelines.

Channel selection and management require strategic consideration during overlapping crises. Different audiences may need different communication channels, yet messages must remain consistent across all platforms. Social media, traditional news outlets, emergency alert systems, and community networks all play vital roles in comprehensive crisis communication.

Timing and frequency of communications demand careful calibration when multiple crises compete for attention. Too many messages can overwhelm audiences, while too few may leave critical information gaps. Regular scheduling of updates helps manage expectations and maintain public engagement without causing information overload.

Cultural sensitivity becomes particularly important when crises affect diverse communities simultaneously. Messages must be tailored to different cultural contexts while maintaining consistency in core information. Translation services, cultural liaisons, and community partnerships help ensure effective communication across different populations.

Visual communication tools help convey complex information about multiple crises clearly. Maps, infographics, and data visualizations can illustrate how different emergencies interact and affect communities. These tools must be designed for quick comprehension while maintaining accuracy and relevance.

Rumor management takes on increased importance during overlapping crises. Misinformation can spread rapidly when multiple emergencies create confusion and anxiety. Establishing fact-checking mechanisms and rapid response protocols helps maintain message integrity and public trust.

Spokesperson coordination becomes essential when multiple crises require different expert voices. Health officials, emergency managers, and technical specialists must align their messages while speaking within their areas of expertise. Regular briefings between spokespersons help maintain consistency across different crisis communications.

Feedback mechanisms help organizations adjust their communication strategies as situations evolve. Monitoring public response, tracking message effectiveness, and gathering community input allows for real-time adjustment of communication approaches. These mechanisms must function across all active crisis situations.

Internal communication requires particular attention during overlapping crises. Staff members need clear information about how different emergencies affect their roles and responsibilities. Regular updates help maintain organizational alignment and effective response capabilities.

Message archives become valuable resources for managing ongoing communications during extended crises. Maintaining accessible records of previous communications helps ensure consistency over time while providing context for new developments. These archives must be well-organized and easily searchable.

Technology platforms must be managed strategically to support multiple crisis communications. Emergency notification systems, public information websites, and social media management tools must handle increased demands while maintaining reliability. Backup systems help ensure continuous communication capabilities.

Community engagement strategies take on added importance during overlapping crises. Local leaders, community organizations, and neighborhood networks help extend official communications and provide valuable feedback. These partnerships strengthen crisis communication effectiveness across different emergency situations.

Message testing becomes crucial when dealing with complex crisis communications. Pilot messaging with focus groups or community representatives helps ensure clarity and effectiveness before wide distribution. This testing must account for how different audiences might interpret messages about multiple crises.

Resource allocation for communications requires careful planning during overlapping emergencies. Staff time, technical capabilities, and communication budgets must be distributed effectively across different crisis response efforts. Clear priorities help guide resource allocation decisions.

Recovery communications need integration into ongoing crisis messaging. As some emergencies begin to resolve, communications must address both immediate crisis needs and longer-term recovery concerns. This requires careful balance between maintaining crisis awareness and building hope for recovery.

Future planning for crisis communications must account for the increasing likelihood of overlapping emergencies. Organizations need flexible communication strategies that can adapt to multiple simultaneous crises while maintaining effectiveness. Regular review and updating of communication plans helps build this capability.

Success in crisis communication during overlapping emergencies ultimately depends on building robust systems and capabilities before crises occur. Organizations must invest in training, technology, and relationships that support effective communication across multiple emergency situations. Regular testing and refinement of communication strategies helps prepare for complex crisis scenarios.

Adaptive Leadership in Unstable Environments

Leadership during periods of instability requires a unique blend of flexibility, decisiveness, and emotional intelligence. When environments shift rapidly and unpredictably, traditional leadership approaches often prove insufficient, demanding instead a more dynamic and responsive style that can navigate through uncertainty while maintaining organizational cohesion.

The essence of adaptive leadership lies in recognizing patterns within chaos while remaining open to new information and changing circumstances. During the 2008 financial crisis, successful leaders demonstrated this capability by quickly adjusting their strategies as market conditions evolved, while maintaining clear vision and purpose for their organizations.

Decision-making under uncertainty becomes a critical skill in unstable environments. Leaders must balance the need for quick action with thoughtful analysis, often making crucial choices with incomplete information. The most effective leaders develop frameworks that allow for rapid decision-making while maintaining flexibility to adjust as situations change.

Emotional resilience proves essential when leading through instability. Leaders must manage their own stress and anxiety while supporting their teams through uncertain times. This requires developing strong self-awareness and maintaining physical and mental well-being despite intense pressures.

Team dynamics take on heightened importance during unstable periods. Leaders must foster environments where teams feel safe expressing concerns while maintaining focus on objectives. Building trust becomes paramount, as teams need confidence in leadership during times of uncertainty.

Communication patterns must adapt to changing circumstances while maintaining clarity and consistency. Successful leaders develop multiple channels for information flow, ensuring critical messages reach all levels of their organization while remaining responsive to feedback and emerging concerns.

Strategic thinking requires particular flexibility in unstable environments. Rather than rigid long-term plans, leaders must develop adaptive strategies that can evolve with changing circumstances while maintaining core organizational values and objectives. This approach allows for quick pivots while preserving strategic direction.

Resource management becomes more complex during periods of instability. Leaders must make difficult allocation decisions while maintaining reserves for unexpected challenges. This requires developing sophisticated monitoring systems and maintaining close awareness of resource utilization patterns.

Relationship building takes on new importance in unstable environments. Leaders must nurture networks of support and collaboration that can provide resources and assistance during difficult times. These relationships often prove crucial for navigating through periods of intense challenge.

Innovation and creativity become essential leadership tools during instability. Leaders must encourage new approaches while maintaining sufficient structure to ensure effective operations. This balance between creativity and control often determines success in managing through uncertain times.

Risk assessment requires continuous updating in unstable environments. Leaders must regularly reassess threats and opportunities as conditions change, adjusting their approaches accordingly. This dynamic risk management approach helps organizations navigate through uncertainty while maintaining operational effectiveness.

Cultural sensitivity becomes particularly important when leading across different contexts during instability. Leaders must adapt their approaches to various cultural expectations while maintaining consistent core principles. This flexibility helps build trust and cooperation across diverse stakeholder groups.

Technology utilization must balance innovation with reliability in unstable environments. Leaders need to leverage new tools and capabilities while ensuring essential systems remain functional. This requires careful evaluation of technology investments and maintenance of robust backup systems.

Performance management takes on new dimensions during instability. Leaders must adjust metrics and expectations while maintaining accountability and motivation. This requires developing flexible assessment approaches that account for changing circumstances while supporting continuous improvement.

Succession planning becomes crucial in unstable environments. Leaders must prepare their organizations for leadership transitions while maintaining current operational effectiveness. This includes developing multiple layers of leadership capability throughout the organization.

Learning agility distinguishes successful leaders in unstable environments. The ability to quickly absorb new information and adapt approaches proves essential for navigating through uncertainty. Leaders must model this learning orientation while encouraging similar flexibility throughout their organizations.

Future orientation remains important despite immediate challenges. Leaders must maintain focus on long-term objectives while managing current instability. This requires developing robust scenario planning capabilities and maintaining strategic perspective despite tactical pressures.

Success in unstable environments ultimately depends on building organizational capabilities that support adaptive leadership. This includes developing strong teams, flexible systems, and resilient cultures that can thrive despite uncertainty. Regular testing and refinement of these capabilities helps organizations prepare for future challenges.

The most effective leaders in unstable environments combine personal adaptability with strong organizational systems. They maintain clear vision while remaining flexible in execution, support their teams while demanding excellence, and balance immediate needs with long-term objectives. This comprehensive approach helps organizations navigate through periods of instability while emerging stronger and more capable.

Chapter 4: Institutional Resilience

Building Adaptive Governance Systems

Adaptive governance systems represent the cornerstone of resilient organizations capable of responding to rapidly changing circumstances while maintaining operational effectiveness. These systems must balance stability with flexibility, enabling quick responses to emerging challenges while preserving core institutional functions and values.

The foundation of adaptive governance lies in creating structures that can evolve without losing their essential purpose. During the aftermath of Hurricane Katrina, communities that successfully rebuilt demonstrated this principle by developing new coordination mechanisms while maintaining traditional democratic processes. These hybrid approaches proved more effective than rigid pre-existing systems.

Decision-making frameworks within adaptive governance must support both rapid response and thoughtful deliberation. Organizations need clear protocols for emergency decisions while maintaining processes for longer-term planning and stakeholder engagement. The Dutch water management system exemplifies this balance, combining quick-response capabilities with extensive community consultation.

Information flow becomes crucial in adaptive systems. Governance structures must facilitate rapid sharing of critical data while ensuring accuracy and appropriate distribution. This requires developing multiple communication channels and establishing clear protocols for information verification and dissemination.

Stakeholder engagement takes on new importance in adaptive governance. Systems must incorporate diverse perspectives while maintaining ability to act decisively when needed. Successful models often include multiple layers of participation, from core decision-making groups to broader advisory networks.

Resource allocation mechanisms need particular flexibility in adaptive systems. Governance structures must support quick redeployment of resources while maintaining accountability and oversight. This requires developing sophisticated tracking systems and clear authority frameworks for resource decisions.

Learning mechanisms become essential components of adaptive governance. Systems must incorporate feedback loops that allow for continuous improvement and adjustment based on experience. Regular review processes help organizations identify successful approaches and necessary modifications.

Cultural elements play vital roles in adaptive governance. Systems must align with local values and practices while maintaining capability for change when needed. This cultural sensitivity helps build trust and support for governance mechanisms across different stakeholder groups.

Technology integration requires careful consideration in adaptive systems. Governance structures must leverage new capabilities while maintaining reliability and accessibility. This includes developing backup systems and ensuring technology supports rather than constrains adaptive capacity.

Accountability mechanisms need redesign for adaptive contexts. Traditional compliance-based approaches often prove too rigid, while complete flexibility risks losing essential controls. Successful systems develop new metrics that balance accountability with adaptability.

Coordination across different scales presents particular challenges in adaptive governance. Systems must facilitate cooperation between local, regional, and national levels while maintaining clear lines of authority. The European Union's subsidiary principle demonstrates how different governance levels can work together effectively.

Risk management takes on new dimensions in adaptive systems. Governance structures must balance prevention with response capability, developing approaches that address both known and emerging risks. This requires sophisticated monitoring systems and flexible response protocols.

Leadership development becomes crucial for adaptive governance. Systems must nurture leaders capable of operating effectively in uncertain environments while maintaining institutional stability. This includes creating opportunities for emerging leaders to gain experience with adaptive approaches.

Financial mechanisms need particular attention in adaptive systems. Governance structures must maintain fiscal responsibility while ensuring resources for rapid response when needed. This often requires developing new funding models that combine stability with flexibility.

Performance assessment requires rethinking in adaptive contexts. Traditional metrics often prove inadequate for measuring effectiveness in rapidly changing environments. New evaluation approaches must consider both immediate results and long-term adaptive capacity.

Network development plays a vital role in adaptive governance. Systems must build and maintain relationships that can provide support and resources during challenging times. These networks often prove crucial for successful adaptation to new circumstances.

Future orientation remains essential in adaptive systems. Governance structures must maintain long-term perspective while handling immediate challenges. This requires developing robust planning processes that can adjust to changing conditions while maintaining strategic direction.

Implementation of adaptive governance demands careful attention to local context. Systems must reflect specific organizational and community needs while incorporating broader best practices. Successful implementation often occurs through phased approaches that allow for learning and adjustment.

The success of adaptive governance ultimately depends on building organizational cultures that support flexibility while maintaining stability. This requires consistent effort to develop both structures and capabilities that enable effective response to change while preserving essential functions and values. Regular testing and refinement of governance mechanisms helps ensure continued effectiveness in facing future challenges.

Sustainable adaptive governance emerges from the careful integration of these various elements into coherent systems that can evolve while maintaining core purposes. Organizations must invest in developing these capabilities before major challenges arise, ensuring they can respond effectively when needed. This proactive approach helps build resilient institutions capable of thriving in uncertain environments.

Strengthening International Cooperation Frameworks

International cooperation frameworks serve as vital mechanisms for addressing global challenges that transcend national boundaries. The interconnected nature of modern crises demands sophisticated approaches to collaboration that can overcome traditional barriers while respecting national sovereignty and cultural differences.

Historical examples demonstrate the power of effective international cooperation. The Montreal Protocol's success in addressing ozone depletion showed how nations could work together to solve complex environmental challenges. This framework provided a template for future collaborative efforts, highlighting the importance of shared scientific understanding and graduated implementation schedules.

Trust-building represents a fundamental element of successful international cooperation. Nations must develop confidence in their partners' commitments while maintaining transparency in their own actions. The European Union's early development illustrated how former adversaries could build trust through incremental cooperation on specific issues.

Decision-making processes in international frameworks require careful design to balance efficiency with inclusivity. The World Health Organization's response mechanisms demonstrate how international bodies can make rapid decisions while maintaining broad consultation and support. These processes must accommodate different national priorities while enabling timely action.

Resource sharing agreements form crucial components of cooperation frameworks. Nations must develop fair and transparent systems for sharing both material and knowledge resources. The International Space Station project exemplifies how countries can pool resources effectively while maintaining individual contributions and benefits.

Communication systems need particular attention in international contexts. Frameworks must support clear information exchange across language and cultural barriers while maintaining accuracy and security. The development of standardized protocols helps ensure effective communication during critical situations.

Cultural sensitivity plays a vital role in international cooperation. Frameworks must acknowledge and respect different cultural approaches while building common ground for action. Successful programs often incorporate cultural liaison roles and multilingual capabilities to facilitate understanding.

Technology platforms require careful consideration in international frameworks. Systems must be accessible across different technical capabilities while maintaining security and reliability. Common standards and interoperability protocols help ensure effective technological cooperation.

Dispute resolution mechanisms prove essential for maintaining cooperative relationships. Frameworks must include clear processes for addressing disagreements while preserving overall collaboration. The World Trade Organization's dispute settlement system provides valuable lessons in managing international conflicts constructively.

Capacity building becomes crucial for effective international cooperation. Stronger partners must support development of capabilities in less-resourced nations while respecting local autonomy. This investment in shared capacity helps ensure more effective global responses to common challenges.

Monitoring and evaluation systems need adaptation for international contexts. Frameworks must track progress and effectiveness across different national systems while maintaining comparable standards. Regular assessment helps identify areas for improvement and adaptation.

Financial mechanisms require particular attention in international cooperation. Frameworks must ensure fair distribution of costs and benefits while maintaining accountability for resource use. The Green Climate Fund demonstrates how complex financial arrangements can support international cooperation.

Leadership development takes on added importance in international contexts. Frameworks must nurture leaders capable of working effectively across cultural and national boundaries while maintaining domestic support. This includes creating opportunities for emerging leaders to gain international experience.

Risk management strategies must account for diverse national perspectives. Frameworks need to balance different risk tolerances while maintaining effective collective action. This requires sophisticated assessment tools and flexible response mechanisms.

Knowledge sharing systems prove vital for international cooperation. Frameworks must facilitate exchange of expertise and experience while protecting intellectual property rights. Successful programs often include multiple channels for knowledge transfer and joint learning.

Implementation planning requires careful attention to national differences. Frameworks must accommodate varying capabilities and circumstances while maintaining progress toward common goals. Phased approaches often help manage these differences effectively.

Future orientation becomes essential in international cooperation. Frameworks must maintain long-term perspective while addressing immediate challenges. This requires developing shared visions that can inspire sustained commitment across national boundaries.

Network development plays a crucial role in strengthening international cooperation. Frameworks must build and maintain relationships at multiple levels, from technical experts to political leaders. These networks often prove vital during crisis response and program implementation.

Success in international cooperation ultimately depends on building frameworks that can evolve while maintaining core purposes. Nations must invest in developing these capabilities before major challenges arise, ensuring they can respond effectively when needed. Regular review and refinement of cooperation mechanisms helps ensure continued effectiveness in addressing global challenges.

The most effective international cooperation frameworks combine clear structures with flexible implementation approaches. They maintain strong commitment to shared goals while accommodating national differences, support rapid response while ensuring broad consultation, and balance immediate needs with long-term objectives. This comprehensive approach helps build resilient international systems capable of addressing complex global challenges.

Chapter 5: Case Studies in Cascade Diplomacy

The 2008 Financial Crisis and Its Diplomatic Aftermath

The global financial crisis of 2008 fundamentally reshaped international diplomatic relations and economic governance structures. What began as a collapse in the U.S. housing market rapidly transformed into a worldwide economic catastrophe that tested existing diplomatic frameworks and forced nations to reconsider their approaches to financial cooperation.

Wall Street's collapse in September 2008 sent shockwaves through global markets, triggering a cascade of failures that exposed the deep interconnections of the modern financial system. As Lehman Brothers filed for bankruptcy, diplomatic channels suddenly became critical lifelines for preventing total economic collapse. Finance ministers and central bank governors engaged in unprecedented levels of coordination, often conducting emergency conferences at odd hours to address rapidly evolving situations.

The creation of the G20 Leaders' Summit marked a pivotal moment in crisis response. Previously a relatively minor ministerial-level meeting, it evolved into the premier forum for international economic cooperation. This transformation reflected a crucial recognition that the existing G7 framework could no longer adequately address global economic challenges without including emerging economies like China, India, and Brazil.

Diplomatic tensions emerged as nations struggled to balance domestic political pressures with international cooperation needs. The United States faced criticism for exporting its financial crisis globally, while European nations grappled with internal divisions over response strategies. China's massive stimulus package demonstrated its growing economic influence, shifting traditional power dynamics in international negotiations.

The crisis revealed significant gaps in global financial governance. The International Monetary Fund, despite its central role in crisis response, faced questions about its legitimacy and effectiveness. This led to major reforms in IMF voting rights and governance structures, reflecting the changing balance of global economic power.

Regulatory cooperation underwent substantial evolution following the crisis. The Financial Stability Board emerged as a key coordinator of international financial regulations, while the Basel Committee on Banking Supervision developed more stringent capital requirements for banks. These changes required delicate diplomatic negotiations to balance national sovereignty with global stability needs.

The European sovereign debt crisis, a direct aftermath of 2008, tested diplomatic relationships within the European Union. Greece's near-default in 2010 sparked intense negotiations between European partners, the IMF, and private creditors. The crisis strained the EU's political fabric, revealing deep divisions between northern and southern member states over financial responsibility and solidarity.

Emerging markets gained unprecedented influence in global economic diplomacy. Brazil, Russia, India, China, and South Africa (BRICS) established new institutions like the New Development Bank, challenging the traditional dominance of Western-led financial institutions. This shift required established powers to adapt their diplomatic approaches and accept new voices in global economic governance.

Trade relationships faced significant pressures as nations grappled with recovery strategies. While some countries advocated for increased protectionism, others pushed for maintaining open markets. The G20's pledge to resist protectionist measures became a crucial test of international cooperation, though implementation proved challenging.

The crisis spurred innovation in diplomatic mechanisms for crisis prevention and response. Central bank swap lines, initially established as emergency measures, became permanent features of the international financial architecture. These arrangements required careful diplomatic negotiation to ensure fairness and effectiveness while maintaining national autonomy.

Public diplomacy took on new importance as governments struggled to explain complex financial interventions to their citizens. Leaders had to balance technical economic solutions with political feasibility, often leading to complicated compromises in international agreements.

The aftermath of 2008 saw a fundamental shift in how nations approach financial diplomacy. Regular stress testing of banks became standard practice internationally, requiring unprecedented sharing of sensitive financial information between countries. This cooperation required building new trust relationships and information-sharing protocols.

Regional financial arrangements gained prominence as complements to global institutions. The Chiang Mai Initiative in Asia and the European Stability Mechanism represented new approaches to regional financial cooperation, though their development required careful diplomatic navigation to avoid undermining global frameworks.

The crisis also transformed how nations approach economic surveillance. The IMF's Financial Sector Assessment Program expanded significantly, while the G20's Mutual Assessment Process created new mechanisms for monitoring global economic imbalances. These changes required sophisticated diplomatic efforts to overcome sovereignty concerns.

A decade after the crisis, its diplomatic impact continues to influence international relations. The rise of digital currencies, financial technology, and new forms of economic cooperation all reflect lessons learned from 2008. Nations now approach financial diplomacy with greater awareness of systemic risks and the need for coordinated responses.

The 2008 crisis demonstrated that effective international cooperation requires both formal institutions and informal diplomatic networks. The relationships built during the crisis response continue to facilitate international economic cooperation, though maintaining these connections requires ongoing diplomatic investment.

Success in preventing future crises depends on maintaining and strengthening the diplomatic frameworks developed since 2008. This requires sustained commitment to international cooperation, even as memories of the crisis fade and new challenges emerge. The lessons learned from this period remain crucial for addressing future global economic challenges.

COVID 19 and Global Response Mechanisms

The COVID-19 pandemic emerged as an unprecedented test of global health security systems and international cooperation mechanisms. When initial reports of a novel coronavirus surfaced in late 2019, few could have predicted the profound transformation of global society and international relations that would follow.

Early warning systems demonstrated both strengths and critical weaknesses during the pandemic's initial phase. While scientific networks quickly identified and sequenced the virus, delays in information sharing and political hesitation hindered effective early response. The experience highlighted the need for more robust and independent alert mechanisms that can transcend political considerations.

International health organizations faced extraordinary challenges in coordinating global response efforts. The World Health Organization's declaration of a Public Health Emergency of International Concern in January 2020 marked a crucial moment, yet subsequent actions revealed limitations in existing frameworks for managing global health crises.

Supply chain disruptions emerged as a critical vulnerability in the global response. Countries scrambled to secure essential medical supplies, often competing against each other and undermining cooperative frameworks. This experience prompted serious reconsideration of critical supply chain management and the need for more resilient international distribution systems.

Vaccine development and distribution highlighted both the potential and limitations of international cooperation. While unprecedented scientific collaboration accelerated vaccine development, inequitable distribution patterns revealed deep-seated global inequalities. The COVAX initiative, despite its limitations, represented an innovative attempt to ensure more equitable vaccine access.

Data sharing mechanisms underwent rapid evolution during the pandemic. Countries developed new protocols for sharing epidemiological information, though political considerations sometimes impeded transparent communication. The experience demonstrated the need for standardized reporting systems that can maintain scientific integrity under political pressure.

Border management policies revealed the tension between national sovereignty and global public health needs. Countries adopted widely varying approaches to travel restrictions, often with limited coordination. This fragmented response highlighted the need for more coherent international frameworks for managing cross-border movement during health crises.

Economic response measures demonstrated the interconnected nature of modern global systems. Central banks and finance ministries coordinated unprecedented support programs, while international financial institutions developed new mechanisms for supporting vulnerable economies. These efforts required innovative approaches to international cooperation.

Public health communication strategies varied significantly across countries, often with dramatic consequences for pandemic outcomes. The spread of misinformation posed particular challenges, requiring new approaches to international information sharing and public education. Social media platforms became crucial battlegrounds in the fight against "infodemic" conditions.

Scientific collaboration reached new levels of intensity and speed during the pandemic. Researchers shared data and findings at unprecedented rates, while new platforms facilitated rapid peer review and information dissemination. This experience created new models for international scientific cooperation.

Healthcare system capacity emerged as a critical factor in pandemic response. Countries with robust public health infrastructure generally fared better, though even well-resourced systems faced severe strains. The experience highlighted the need for sustained investment in global health security.

International aid mechanisms underwent significant adaptation during the crisis. Traditional donor-recipient relationships evolved as countries faced common challenges, requiring new approaches to mutual support and resource sharing. The pandemic demonstrated the limitations of conventional aid models in addressing global challenges.

Technology played a crucial role in pandemic response, from contact tracing apps to virtual meeting platforms. International cooperation in technological development and deployment became increasingly important, though privacy concerns and digital divides posed significant challenges.

Mental health emerged as a crucial consideration in pandemic response. The global nature of lockdowns and social distancing measures created unprecedented psychological challenges, requiring new approaches to international mental health support and cooperation.

Recovery planning highlighted the need for more integrated approaches to global challenges. Countries recognized that effective pandemic recovery required addressing multiple interconnected issues, from health systems strengthening to economic resilience and social support.

Leadership dynamics evolved significantly during the crisis. Traditional power relationships shifted as countries' relative success in pandemic management influenced their global standing. New forms of leadership emerged, often centered on technical expertise and effective crisis management.

Future preparedness became a central focus of international discussion. Countries began developing new frameworks for preventing and responding to future pandemics, incorporating lessons learned from COVID-19. These efforts emphasized the need for sustained investment in global health security.

The pandemic demonstrated that effective global response mechanisms require both formal structures and informal networks. Success in addressing future health crises will depend on maintaining and strengthening these mechanisms while addressing identified weaknesses. The experience of COVID-19 provides crucial lessons for building more resilient international response systems.

Sustainable solutions must balance national interests with global public health needs. Countries must invest in shared capabilities while maintaining flexibility to address local conditions. This balanced approach helps ensure effective response to future global health challenges while respecting national sovereignty and local contexts.

Climate Change as a Crisis Multiplier

Climate change stands as a profound force that amplifies existing global challenges, transforming localized issues into complex, interconnected crises. The ripple effects of rising temperatures, extreme weather events, and shifting precipitation patterns cascade through social, economic, and political systems, creating unprecedented challenges for communities worldwide.

In regions already grappling with resource scarcity, climate-induced changes exacerbate competition for water, arable land, and essential resources. The Horn of Africa provides a stark example, where recurring droughts intensify conflicts between pastoral communities and accelerate rural-urban migration. These environmental pressures transform traditional disagreements into more severe confrontations, straining local governance systems and international aid mechanisms.

Security implications emerge as climate impacts destabilize vulnerable regions. The Sahel demonstrates how environmental degradation compounds existing tensions, contributing to the rise of extremist groups and forcing mass population movements. Military planners increasingly recognize climate change as a threat multiplier that complicates peacekeeping operations and regional stability efforts.

Food security faces mounting pressure as climate variability disrupts agricultural systems. Changes in growing seasons and increased frequency of extreme weather events threaten crop yields, while rising temperatures affect livestock productivity. These agricultural challenges ripple through global food markets, potentially triggering price spikes and social unrest in import-dependent nations.

Coastal communities confront escalating risks as sea levels rise and storms intensify. Small island nations face existential threats, while populous coastal cities grapple with infrastructure vulnerabilities and potential population displacement. These challenges strain international legal frameworks, raising questions about sovereignty and citizenship for potentially displaced populations.

Economic systems experience cascading effects as climate impacts disrupt supply chains and damage infrastructure. Insurance markets struggle to adapt to increasing disaster frequency, while industries dependent on stable weather patterns face growing uncertainty. These economic pressures can trigger broader market instability and affect global financial systems.

Public health systems face compounded challenges as climate change alters disease patterns and environmental conditions. Vector-borne diseases expand into new regions, while extreme weather events strain emergency response capabilities. These health impacts often disproportionately affect vulnerable populations, exacerbating existing social inequities.

Urban infrastructure confronts multiple pressures as climate impacts stress systems designed for different conditions. Heat waves tax power grids, while flooding challenges drainage systems. These infrastructure strains particularly affect rapidly growing cities in developing regions, where resources for adaptation remain limited.

Migration patterns shift as environmental changes render certain areas less habitable. Climate-induced movement interacts with existing migration pressures, creating complex humanitarian challenges and potential political tensions in receiving regions. Traditional frameworks for managing migration prove inadequate for addressing these emerging patterns.

Biodiversity loss accelerates as climate change disrupts ecosystems and compounds existing environmental pressures. Species extinction rates increase, while ecosystem services vital for human communities deteriorate. These biological impacts create feedback loops that can further intensify climate effects.

Water resources face multiple challenges as changing precipitation patterns affect availability and quality. Competition for water intensifies between agricultural, industrial, and urban users, while transboundary water management becomes more complex. These water pressures can trigger broader regional tensions and affect international relations.

Energy systems require transformation precisely when climate impacts strain existing infrastructure. The need to reduce emissions while maintaining reliable power supplies creates complex technical and political challenges. This energy transition affects international relations and economic systems at multiple levels.

Governance systems face increasing pressure as climate impacts require more complex and coordinated responses. Local governments struggle with immediate adaptation needs, while international frameworks grapple with global mitigation efforts. These governance challenges often reveal and exacerbate existing institutional weaknesses.

Indigenous communities experience particularly severe effects as climate change threatens traditional lifestyles and cultural practices. Traditional knowledge systems offer valuable insights for adaptation, yet often receive insufficient recognition in formal response strategies.

Financial systems confront new risks as climate impacts affect asset values and investment patterns. Insurance markets evolve, while investors increasingly consider climate risks in decision-making. These financial adjustments can create broader economic ripple effects and influence development patterns.

Addressing these multiplied crises requires integrated approaches that recognize interconnections between environmental, social, and economic systems. Success depends on strengthening resilience at multiple levels while addressing underlying vulnerabilities. International cooperation becomes increasingly crucial as climate impacts transcend national boundaries and traditional response capabilities.

The role of climate change as a crisis multiplier demands new approaches to risk assessment and management. Traditional security frameworks must expand to incorporate environmental factors, while development strategies need to prioritize climate resilience. These adapted approaches help communities and nations prepare for increasingly complex challenges while building capacity for effective response.

Cyber Threats and International Security

Climate change stands as a profound force that amplifies existing global challenges, transforming localized issues into complex, interconnected crises. The ripple effects of rising temperatures, extreme weather events, and shifting precipitation patterns cascade through social, economic, and political systems, creating unprecedented challenges for communities worldwide.

In regions already grappling with resource scarcity, climate-induced changes exacerbate competition for water, arable land, and essential resources. The Horn of Africa provides a stark example, where recurring droughts intensify conflicts between pastoral communities and accelerate rural-urban migration. These environmental pressures transform traditional disagreements into more severe confrontations, straining local governance systems and international aid mechanisms.

Security implications emerge as climate impacts destabilize vulnerable regions. The Sahel demonstrates how environmental degradation compounds existing tensions, contributing to the rise of extremist groups and forcing mass population movements. Military planners increasingly recognize climate change as a threat multiplier that complicates peacekeeping operations and regional stability efforts.

Food security faces mounting pressure as climate variability disrupts agricultural systems. Changes in growing seasons and increased frequency of extreme weather events threaten crop yields, while rising temperatures affect livestock productivity. These agricultural challenges ripple through global food markets, potentially triggering price spikes and social unrest in import-dependent nations.

Coastal communities confront escalating risks as sea levels rise and storms intensify. Small island nations face existential threats, while populous coastal cities grapple with infrastructure vulnerabilities and potential population displacement. These challenges strain international legal frameworks, raising questions about sovereignty and citizenship for potentially displaced populations.

Economic systems experience cascading effects as climate impacts disrupt supply chains and damage infrastructure. Insurance markets struggle to adapt to increasing disaster frequency, while industries dependent on stable weather patterns face growing uncertainty. These economic pressures can trigger broader market instability and affect global financial systems.

Public health systems face compounded challenges as climate change alters disease patterns and environmental conditions. Vector-borne diseases expand into new regions, while extreme weather events strain emergency response capabilities. These health impacts often disproportionately affect vulnerable populations, exacerbating existing social inequities.

Urban infrastructure confronts multiple pressures as climate impacts stress systems designed for different conditions. Heat waves tax power grids, while flooding challenges drainage systems. These infrastructure strains particularly affect rapidly growing cities in developing regions, where resources for adaptation remain limited.

Migration patterns shift as environmental changes render certain areas less habitable. Climate-induced movement interacts with existing migration pressures, creating complex humanitarian challenges and potential political tensions in receiving regions. Traditional frameworks for managing migration prove inadequate for addressing these emerging patterns.

Biodiversity loss accelerates as climate change disrupts ecosystems and compounds existing environmental pressures. Species extinction rates increase, while ecosystem services vital for human communities deteriorate. These biological impacts create feedback loops that can further intensify climate effects.

Water resources face multiple challenges as changing precipitation patterns affect availability and quality. Competition for water intensifies between agricultural, industrial, and urban users, while transboundary water management becomes more complex. These water pressures can trigger broader regional tensions and affect international relations.

Energy systems require transformation precisely when climate impacts strain existing infrastructure. The need to reduce emissions while maintaining reliable power supplies creates complex technical and political challenges. This energy transition affects international relations and economic systems at multiple levels.

Governance systems face increasing pressure as climate impacts require more complex and coordinated responses. Local governments struggle with immediate adaptation needs, while international frameworks grapple with global mitigation efforts. These governance challenges often reveal and exacerbate existing institutional weaknesses.

Indigenous communities experience particularly severe effects as climate change threatens traditional lifestyles and cultural practices. Traditional knowledge systems offer valuable insights for adaptation, yet often receive insufficient recognition in formal response strategies.

Financial systems confront new risks as climate impacts affect asset values and investment patterns. Insurance markets evolve, while investors increasingly consider climate risks in decision-making. These financial adjustments can create broader economic ripple effects and influence development patterns.

Addressing these multiplied crises requires integrated approaches that recognize interconnections between environmental, social, and economic systems. Success depends on strengthening resilience at multiple levels while addressing underlying vulnerabilities. International cooperation becomes increasingly crucial as climate impacts transcend national boundaries and traditional response capabilities.

The role of climate change as a crisis multiplier demands new approaches to risk assessment and management. Traditional security frameworks must expand to incorporate environmental factors, while development strategies need to prioritize climate resilience. These adapted approaches help communities and nations prepare for increasingly complex challenges while building capacity for effective response.

Migration Crises and Regional Stability

Mass population movements have emerged as one of the most complex challenges facing the international community, fundamentally reshaping regional dynamics and testing established diplomatic frameworks. The increasing scale and frequency of migration crises create ripple effects that transform social, economic, and political landscapes across multiple regions.

Syria's civil war triggered one of the most significant migration events in recent history, sending millions of people fleeing across borders and challenging the capacity of neighboring states. Turkey, Lebanon, and Jordan faced unprecedented pressures on their infrastructure and social services, while European nations grappled with political upheaval as asylum seekers arrived in growing numbers. This crisis revealed the limitations of existing refugee protection systems and sparked intense debates about responsibility sharing among nations.

The Mediterranean Sea became a focal point of human tragedy as desperate individuals risked treacherous crossings in search of safety and opportunity. Maritime rescue operations highlighted tensions between humanitarian obligations and border control priorities, while human trafficking networks exploited the situation. These challenges forced a reconsideration of regional cooperation mechanisms and border management strategies.

Central America's Northern Triangle experiences persistent migration pressures as violence, poverty, and environmental degradation drive people northward. Mexico finds itself in a complex position, simultaneously serving as a transit country, destination, and source of migrants. This situation strains diplomatic relations throughout the region and tests the capacity of asylum systems.

Climate-induced displacement adds another layer of complexity to migration patterns. Pacific Island nations face existential threats from rising sea levels, while drought and desertification in the Sahel region force traditional communities to abandon ancestral lands. These environmental pressures create new categories of migrants that existing legal frameworks struggle to address.

Border communities often bear the initial impact of migration surges, experiencing rapid demographic changes and resource pressures. These localities require significant support to maintain stability and provide adequate services, yet often lack sufficient resources or institutional capacity. Their experiences demonstrate the importance of multi-level governance approaches to migration management.

Refugee camps, initially conceived as temporary solutions, frequently become semi-permanent settlements that transform local landscapes and economies. The Dadaab complex in Kenya exemplifies how these settlements can alter regional dynamics, creating both challenges and opportunities for host communities. Long-term displacement situations require innovative approaches that balance humanitarian needs with development objectives.

Urban areas increasingly serve as primary destinations for displaced populations, challenging traditional models of refugee assistance. Cities must adapt services and infrastructure while managing social integration and potential tensions with existing residents. This urbanization of displacement requires new approaches to humanitarian aid and development support.

Labor markets experience significant impacts as migration flows alter workforce dynamics. Some regions benefit from increased labor availability, while others face brain drain as skilled workers depart. These economic effects influence both origin and destination countries, requiring careful policy responses to maximize benefits while minimizing disruptions.

Education systems face particular challenges in addressing the needs of displaced populations while maintaining quality standards for host communities. Language barriers, interrupted schooling, and resource constraints create complex challenges for educators and administrators. Success in this area proves crucial for long-term stability and integration.

Health systems must adapt to serve diverse populations with varying medical needs and cultural expectations. The COVID-19 pandemic highlighted particular vulnerabilities in migrant communities and demonstrated the importance of inclusive health policies for regional public health outcomes.

Social cohesion requires careful attention as communities adapt to demographic changes. Successful integration depends on both practical support measures and efforts to build understanding between newcomers and host populations. Cultural exchanges and community engagement initiatives play crucial roles in maintaining stability.

Security considerations take on new dimensions as large-scale population movements affect regional dynamics. Border management must balance legitimate security concerns with humanitarian obligations, while law enforcement agencies adapt to changing community needs. International cooperation proves essential for addressing associated criminal activities.

Gender dimensions of migration crises require specific attention, as women and girls often face particular vulnerabilities during displacement. Protection mechanisms must address gender-based violence while supporting women's leadership roles in displaced communities. These considerations affect both immediate humanitarian response and longer-term stability efforts.

International aid systems continue evolving to address migration challenges more effectively. Traditional humanitarian responses increasingly integrate development approaches, recognizing the long-term nature of many displacement situations.

This evolution requires new funding mechanisms and coordination structures.

Regional stability ultimately depends on addressing root causes while managing immediate migration pressures. Success requires coordinated action across multiple domains, from conflict prevention to economic development and environmental protection. International cooperation remains essential for developing effective responses to these complex challenges.

The future of regional stability increasingly depends on how effectively societies manage migration pressures while maintaining social cohesion and economic vitality. Building resilient systems capable of adapting to population movements while protecting human rights and dignity represents a crucial challenge for the international community.

Chapter 6: Tools and Techniques for Crisis Management

Digital Diplomacy and Crisis Response

Digital platforms have fundamentally transformed the landscape of international crisis response, creating new channels for diplomatic engagement and reshaping how nations interact during critical moments. Social media platforms, instant messaging, and virtual meeting spaces now serve as essential tools for diplomatic communication, enabling rapid response and real-time coordination during emergencies.

The Iranian protests of 2009 marked an early watershed moment for digital diplomacy, as Twitter became a crucial platform for both protesters and international observers. This event demonstrated the potential for digital tools to bypass traditional diplomatic channels and connect directly with populations in crisis. Since then, diplomatic missions worldwide have developed sophisticated digital strategies to maintain continuous engagement with diverse audiences.

During natural disasters, digital platforms enable unprecedented coordination of international relief efforts. When the 2015 Nepal earthquake struck, social media platforms facilitated immediate communication between affected communities, aid organizations, and diplomatic missions. Embassy Twitter accounts transformed into emergency response centers, sharing critical information and coordinating evacuation efforts.

Virtual embassy platforms have emerged as innovative solutions for maintaining diplomatic presence in high-risk areas. These digital missions allow continued engagement when physical presence becomes impossible, ensuring diplomatic channels remain open during crises. Such platforms proved particularly valuable during periods of political instability or health emergencies.

Real-time monitoring of social media feeds now forms a crucial component of early warning systems for emerging crises. Diplomatic missions analyze digital signals to identify potential flashpoints and coordinate preemptive responses. This capability enables more proactive crisis management and helps prevent escalation of developing situations.

Cybersecurity has become inseparable from crisis diplomacy as digital threats increasingly accompany physical emergencies. Diplomatic missions must now coordinate responses to hybrid threats that combine traditional security challenges with cyber operations. This evolution requires new expertise and cooperation mechanisms among nations.

Digital tools enable more inclusive crisis response by facilitating direct engagement with affected communities. Diplomatic missions can gather real-time feedback from local populations, helping shape more effective and culturally sensitive interventions.

This direct connection helps build trust and improve the effectiveness of crisis response efforts.

Public diplomacy has evolved significantly in the digital age, with social media platforms enabling rapid dissemination of official positions and updates during crises. However, this speed and reach also create challenges in managing misinformation and maintaining message consistency across multiple channels.

Crisis coordination benefits from digital platforms that enable simultaneous communication among multiple stakeholders. Virtual situation rooms allow diplomatic teams from different countries to share information and coordinate responses in real-time, improving the efficiency of international crisis management.

Digital archives provide valuable resources for learning from past crises and improving future responses. These repositories of diplomatic communications, social media interactions, and crisis management decisions help inform training and protocol development for diplomatic missions worldwide.

Privacy and security considerations have become increasingly complex as diplomatic communications move into digital spaces. Missions must balance the need for rapid information sharing with the protection of sensitive data and communications. This challenge requires ongoing adaptation of diplomatic protocols and security measures.

Cultural diplomacy finds new expression through digital platforms during crises, helping maintain international relationships even when physical contact becomes impossible. Virtual cultural exchanges and online events help preserve diplomatic ties and foster understanding during challenging times.

Training for diplomatic personnel now includes extensive digital components, preparing staff for crisis response in an interconnected world. This education covers both technical skills and strategic understanding of how digital tools can support diplomatic objectives during emergencies.

Mobile applications have become essential tools for crisis response, enabling diplomatic missions to reach citizens quickly during emergencies. These apps provide direct communication channels, emergency instructions, and coordination capabilities for evacuation efforts.

Data analytics support more sophisticated crisis response strategies by helping diplomatic missions identify patterns and predict potential developments. This capability enables more targeted interventions and better resource allocation during emergencies.

International cooperation frameworks increasingly incorporate digital components, recognizing the essential role of technology in modern crisis response. These agreements address issues like information sharing protocols and coordination of digital resources during emergencies.

Future challenges in digital diplomacy include adapting to emerging technologies while maintaining diplomatic principles and security. Diplomatic missions must stay ahead of technological developments while ensuring their digital presence remains effective and secure.

The evolution of digital diplomacy continues to reshape international crisis response capabilities. Success in this domain requires balancing technological innovation with traditional diplomatic skills and maintaining human connections despite increasing digitalization. As global challenges become more complex, the effective integration of digital tools into diplomatic practice remains crucial for successful crisis management.

Data Driven Decision Making in Complex Scenarios

Data-driven approaches have revolutionized how leaders and organizations navigate complex scenarios, transforming intuition-based decisions into evidence-supported actions. The integration of vast data sets, advanced analytics, and real-time information flows enables more precise and effective responses to multifaceted challenges.

During the Ebola outbreak in West Africa, health organizations leveraged mobile phone data to track population movements and predict disease spread patterns. This innovative approach allowed authorities to allocate medical resources more effectively and implement targeted containment measures. The success of this method demonstrated how data analytics could enhance traditional emergency response strategies.

Financial markets exemplify the power of data-driven decision making, where algorithms process millions of data points to identify patterns and anticipate market movements. Trading firms analyze everything from social media sentiment to weather patterns, creating sophisticated models that help navigate market volatility and manage risk exposure.

Urban planning has been transformed by the integration of multiple data streams, from traffic patterns to energy consumption. Cities like Barcelona use sensor networks to monitor air quality, pedestrian flow, and waste management in real-time, enabling administrators to make informed decisions about resource allocation and infrastructure development.

Emergency response systems now incorporate diverse data sources to improve disaster management. Satellite imagery, social media feeds, and weather data combine to create comprehensive situational awareness during natural disasters. This integration enables faster, more targeted responses and better coordination among multiple agencies.

Supply chain management demonstrates how data analytics can optimize complex global networks. Companies analyze shipping routes, inventory levels, and market demands to maintain efficient operations despite disruptions. During the global shipping crisis, organizations using advanced analytics adapted more quickly to changing conditions.

Healthcare systems utilize patient data, treatment outcomes, and population health metrics to improve service delivery. Predictive analytics help hospitals anticipate admission rates, optimize staffing levels, and identify high-risk patients requiring preventive interventions. This approach has proven particularly valuable during public health emergencies.

Environmental protection efforts benefit from sophisticated data analysis, combining satellite observations with ground-level measurements to track ecosystem changes. Conservation organizations use this information to identify threatened areas and design more effective protection strategies. The Amazon rainforest monitoring system exemplifies this approach, enabling rapid response to deforestation activities.

Military operations increasingly rely on data-driven decision making to enhance strategic planning and tactical execution. Modern command centers process information from multiple sensors and sources to create comprehensive battlefield awareness. This capability enables more precise and effective operations while minimizing unintended consequences.

Agricultural systems employ data analytics to optimize crop yields and resource usage. Farmers combine weather forecasts, soil moisture measurements, and market data to make planting and harvesting decisions. This precision agriculture approach has proven crucial for adapting to changing climate conditions.

Public policy development benefits from enhanced data analysis capabilities, enabling policymakers to better understand complex social issues. Demographics, economic indicators, and program outcomes data help design more effective interventions and allocate resources more efficiently.

Education systems use learning analytics to personalize instruction and identify students needing additional support. Schools combine attendance records, assessment results, and engagement metrics to create early warning systems for academic challenges. This approach helps educators intervene before problems escalate.

Transportation networks optimize operations through continuous analysis of traffic patterns, weather conditions, and maintenance needs. Smart city initiatives demonstrate how integrated data systems can improve mobility while reducing congestion and emissions.

Energy grid management exemplifies complex scenario handling, balancing supply and demand while incorporating renewable sources. Grid operators analyze weather forecasts, consumption patterns, and equipment status to maintain stable power delivery despite increasing system complexity.

Security operations centers process vast amounts of data to identify and respond to threats. By analyzing network traffic, access patterns, and threat intelligence, organizations can detect and respond to security incidents more effectively. This capability proves essential in protecting critical infrastructure.

Retail operations demonstrate how real-time data analysis can optimize inventory management and customer service. Companies analyze purchase patterns, weather forecasts, and social media trends to anticipate demand and adjust operations accordingly.

The future of data-driven decision making lies in improving our ability to process and interpret increasingly complex data sets while maintaining human oversight and ethical considerations. Success requires balancing automated analysis with human judgment, ensuring decisions remain aligned with organizational values and societal needs.

Organizations must develop robust data governance frameworks to ensure information quality and appropriate use. Privacy protection, data security, and ethical considerations become increasingly important as decision-making systems grow more sophisticated. These foundations support confident decision-making while maintaining public trust and regulatory compliance.

The evolution of data-driven decision making continues to accelerate, enabling more sophisticated responses to complex challenges. Success requires combining technical capabilities with domain expertise and ethical awareness, ensuring decisions serve both organizational objectives and broader societal interests.

Diplomatic Innovation and Technology Integration

Modern diplomacy has undergone a profound transformation through the integration of technological innovations, reshaping how nations interact, negotiate, and resolve conflicts. From secure communication platforms to virtual reality simulations, technology has expanded the toolkit available to diplomatic practitioners while creating new challenges and opportunities.

The evolution of diplomatic practice became strikingly apparent during the global health crisis of 2020, when traditional face-to-face diplomacy suddenly shifted to virtual platforms. This rapid transition demonstrated both the potential and limitations of technology in diplomatic relations, as leaders adapted to conducting sensitive negotiations and maintaining international relationships through digital channels.

Blockchain technology has emerged as a powerful tool for treaty verification and international agreements. By providing immutable records and transparent tracking mechanisms, blockchain applications help build trust between nations while streamlining diplomatic processes. Several countries have begun exploring blockchain-based systems for trade agreements and cross-border transactions.

Virtual reality applications now enable diplomats to experience distant crisis zones or cultural heritage sites without physical travel. These immersive experiences enhance understanding and empathy, crucial elements in conflict resolution and cultural diplomacy. Diplomatic training programs increasingly incorporate VR simulations to prepare practitioners for complex scenarios.

Secure communication platforms have evolved beyond traditional diplomatic cables to include encrypted messaging systems and protected video conferencing. These technologies enable rapid response to emerging situations while maintaining the confidentiality essential to diplomatic exchanges. Modern diplomatic missions operate through layered security protocols that protect sensitive communications while facilitating necessary information sharing.

Environmental monitoring technologies support diplomatic efforts in climate change negotiations. Satellite imagery, sensor networks, and data analytics help verify compliance with international agreements and provide objective evidence for environmental discussions. This technological capability has transformed how nations approach environmental diplomacy and resource management.

Social media analytics tools help diplomatic missions gauge public sentiment and identify emerging issues before they escalate into crises. By monitoring digital conversations and tracking opinion trends, diplomats can better understand local contexts and adjust their approaches accordingly. This capability proves particularly valuable during times of social or political tension.

Translation technologies have reduced language barriers in diplomatic interactions, enabling more inclusive and efficient communication. Real-time translation services support both formal negotiations and informal diplomatic exchanges, though human interpreters remain essential for nuanced discussions and cultural context.

Digital archives and knowledge management systems preserve institutional memory while making diplomatic history more accessible. These resources help diplomats learn from past experiences and apply historical insights to current challenges. Modern diplomatic services invest heavily in developing and maintaining these digital knowledge bases.

Remote sensing technologies provide diplomatic missions with independent verification capabilities for arms control agreements and territorial disputes. These tools support fact-based negotiations and help prevent escalation of conflicts based on disputed information. Satellite imagery has become particularly crucial in monitoring compliance with international agreements.

Cybersecurity has become a central concern in diplomatic operations, requiring continuous technological adaptation and international cooperation. Diplomatic missions must protect their digital infrastructure while engaging in discussions about global cybersecurity norms and responses to cyber threats.

Mobile applications support crisis response and citizen services, enabling diplomatic missions to better serve their nationals abroad. These tools provide real-time updates, emergency assistance, and direct communication channels between missions and citizens in need.

Data visualization tools help diplomats communicate complex information effectively to diverse audiences. These technologies support both internal analysis and public diplomacy efforts, making diplomatic work more transparent and accessible to broader audiences.

Predictive analytics support strategic planning by helping diplomatic services anticipate potential challenges and opportunities. By analyzing historical data and current trends, these tools enhance diplomatic preparedness and resource allocation.

Internet connectivity has become essential diplomatic infrastructure, supporting everything from routine communications to emergency response. Diplomatic missions now require robust digital capabilities to function effectively in the modern world.

Training programs for diplomatic personnel increasingly emphasize technological literacy alongside traditional diplomatic skills. Modern diplomats must understand both the potential and limitations of various technologies while maintaining core diplomatic competencies.

The future of diplomatic innovation lies in balancing technological advancement with human judgment and traditional diplomatic values. Success requires maintaining the personal relationships and trust essential to diplomacy while leveraging technology to enhance capabilities and efficiency.

Integration of new technologies must consider both opportunities and risks, ensuring that innovation serves diplomatic objectives without compromising security or effectiveness. Diplomatic services must remain adaptable while preserving the fundamental principles of diplomatic practice.

The ongoing evolution of diplomatic technology integration continues to reshape international relations. As new tools and capabilities emerge, the challenge remains to harness these innovations in ways that enhance diplomatic practice while preserving its essential human elements.

Chapter 7: Future Perspectives

Emerging Trends in Crisis Diplomacy

Crisis diplomacy has evolved dramatically in recent years, shaped by technological advances, changing global power dynamics, and new forms of international threats. Traditional diplomatic approaches are being supplemented and sometimes replaced by innovative methods that respond to the increasing complexity of modern crises.

The Belarus-Poland border crisis of 2021 exemplified how modern crisis diplomacy must address hybrid threats combining traditional security challenges with information warfare and humanitarian issues. Diplomatic responses now require coordinated action across multiple domains, from social media engagement to economic measures, while maintaining traditional diplomatic channels.

Climate-related diplomatic crises have emerged as a defining challenge, requiring new approaches to international cooperation. The Pacific Island nations' diplomatic initiatives demonstrate how vulnerable states can leverage international forums and digital platforms to build coalitions and advocate for urgent action, transforming traditional power dynamics in crisis negotiations.

Health diplomacy has gained prominence, with pandemics requiring unprecedented levels of international coordination. Nations have developed new protocols for sharing medical data, coordinating research efforts, and managing cross-border health responses. These experiences have created new frameworks for managing future health-related diplomatic crises.

Cyber incidents increasingly trigger diplomatic crises, requiring rapid response capabilities and new forms of international cooperation. States have developed specialized diplomatic units focused on cyber issues, while establishing new channels for technical cooperation during incidents that threaten global digital infrastructure.

Social media has transformed crisis communication, with diplomatic missions now operating as digital first responders during emergencies. Real-time public diplomacy through social platforms has become essential for managing perceptions and countering misinformation during crises, while maintaining diplomatic credibility.

Economic coercion has evolved into a more sophisticated tool of crisis diplomacy, with targeted sanctions and financial measures requiring complex international coordination. Modern diplomatic responses must navigate intricate global financial systems while considering potential unintended consequences and maintaining international support.

Environmental disasters have sparked innovation in diplomatic response mechanisms. The Amazon rainforest fires of 2019 demonstrated how environmental crises now involve multiple stakeholders, requiring diplomats to coordinate with scientific experts, indigenous communities, and environmental organizations while managing international pressure.

Hostage diplomacy has become more complex in an interconnected world, where public pressure through social media can significantly impact negotiations. Diplomatic services have adapted by developing specialized crisis teams that combine traditional negotiation skills with digital communication expertise.

Urban diplomacy has emerged as cities increasingly engage in direct crisis response coordination, bypassing traditional national diplomatic channels. Major cities now maintain their own international networks for managing crises, from climate emergencies to public health challenges.

Diaspora communities play an expanding role in crisis diplomacy, with digital platforms enabling rapid mobilization and influence on diplomatic responses. Modern crisis management must consider these transnational networks and their impact on both home and host country policies.

Technological platforms have enabled new forms of track-two diplomacy during crises, with non-governmental actors maintaining dialogue channels when official relations become strained. These informal diplomatic initiatives often prove crucial in preventing crisis escalation and preparing ground for official negotiations.

Food security crises have prompted innovation in diplomatic coordination, particularly in managing supply chain disruptions and international aid distribution. Digital platforms enable real-time monitoring of food security situations and coordination of multilateral responses.

Refugee crises require increasingly sophisticated diplomatic responses, combining humanitarian coordination with security considerations and long-term planning. Modern approaches emphasize regional cooperation and technology-enabled coordination of resources and information.

Maritime disputes have become more complex, requiring new diplomatic tools for managing tensions and preventing escalation. Satellite technology and digital monitoring systems now support traditional diplomatic mechanisms in maritime crisis management.

Religious and cultural tensions increasingly trigger international crises, requiring diplomatic responses that combine cultural sensitivity with rapid communication capabilities. Modern crisis diplomacy must navigate complex identity politics while maintaining international stability.

The rise of non-state actors has transformed crisis diplomacy, requiring engagement with a broader range of stakeholders during negotiations. Diplomatic services now maintain extensive networks of contacts beyond traditional government channels.

Crisis simulation and training have become more sophisticated, incorporating real-world data and scenario planning tools. Diplomatic services invest heavily in preparing personnel for complex crisis situations through immersive training experiences.

Preventive diplomacy has evolved to incorporate early warning systems and data analytics, enabling more proactive responses to emerging crises. Modern diplomatic services emphasize crisis prevention alongside traditional crisis management.

The future of crisis diplomacy lies in developing more adaptive and resilient response capabilities while maintaining the human relationships essential to effective diplomacy. Success requires combining technological innovation with traditional diplomatic skills and cultural understanding.

Preparing for Future Cascade Scenarios

Cascade scenarios represent complex chains of interconnected events that can rapidly escalate from localized incidents into systemic crises. Understanding and preparing for these scenarios has become crucial as global systems grow increasingly interdependent and vulnerable to cascading failures.

The 2021 Suez Canal blockage demonstrated how a single incident could trigger worldwide supply chain disruptions, affecting industries from automotive manufacturing to retail commerce. This event highlighted the need for robust contingency planning that considers both immediate impacts and long-term ripple effects across global systems.

Financial markets provide numerous examples of cascade scenarios, where the failure of one institution can quickly spread throughout the global financial system. The lessons learned from past financial crises have led to the development of sophisticated early warning systems and stress testing protocols designed to identify potential cascade triggers before they materialize.

Climate-related cascade scenarios pose particular challenges due to their complex interactions between natural and human systems. Rising sea levels can trigger population displacement, which in turn affects food security, political stability, and economic systems. Organizations must develop integrated response frameworks that address multiple interconnected challenges simultaneously.

Infrastructure interdependencies create potential cascade vulnerabilities where failure in one system can rapidly affect others. Power grid failures, for instance, can disrupt water treatment facilities, telecommunications networks, and transportation systems. Modern preparedness strategies must account for these complex dependencies when developing resilience plans.

Supply chain cascade scenarios have become more prevalent as global networks grow more complex. Organizations now employ sophisticated modeling tools to identify potential failure points and develop redundancy strategies. These preparations proved crucial during recent global disruptions, allowing better-prepared organizations to maintain operations despite systemic challenges.

Public health emergencies can trigger cascade effects across healthcare systems, economies, and social structures. Preparing for these scenarios requires coordination across multiple sectors and jurisdictions, with particular attention to maintaining essential services during prolonged crises.

Cybersecurity cascade scenarios present unique challenges due to the interconnected nature of digital systems. Organizations must consider how security breaches might propagate through networks, affecting multiple systems and triggering both technical and operational failures.

Environmental cascade scenarios often develop over extended periods before reaching critical tipping points. Organizations must develop long-term monitoring capabilities to identify early warning signs while maintaining readiness to respond when cascade effects begin to accelerate.

Transportation network disruptions can trigger cascade effects throughout supply chains and urban systems. Preparing for these scenarios requires understanding both physical infrastructure vulnerabilities and the complex web of dependent services and industries.

Social media cascade scenarios can rapidly amplify local events into global crises, requiring new approaches to crisis communication and reputation management. Organizations must develop capabilities to monitor and respond to rapidly evolving narrative cascades while maintaining operational focus.

Resource scarcity scenarios often trigger complex cascade effects across multiple systems. Organizations must prepare for how shortages in key resources might affect their operations while considering potential alternatives and adaptation strategies.

Political instability can create cascade scenarios affecting multiple regions and sectors simultaneously. Preparation requires understanding both direct impacts and potential secondary effects on operations, markets, and stakeholder relationships.

Technological cascade scenarios can emerge from both system failures and rapid technological changes. Organizations must maintain flexibility in their response capabilities while ensuring core systems remain resilient to cascading disruptions.

Natural disaster cascade scenarios require particular attention to geographic vulnerabilities and infrastructure dependencies. Organizations must consider both immediate impact zones and potential cascade effects in surrounding regions and connected systems.

Population movement cascade scenarios can trigger complex social, economic, and political effects across multiple regions. Preparation requires understanding both direct impacts and longer-term implications for social systems and infrastructure needs.

Energy system cascade scenarios can affect multiple dependent systems simultaneously. Organizations must develop comprehensive understanding of their energy dependencies while maintaining backup capabilities for critical operations.

Food system cascade scenarios can trigger complex social and economic effects across regions. Preparation requires understanding both direct supply chain vulnerabilities and potential secondary impacts on social stability and economic systems.

The future of cascade scenario preparation lies in developing more sophisticated modeling capabilities while maintaining flexible response options. Success requires combining technical analysis with practical experience and adaptive management strategies.

Organizations must build resilience through both structural preparations and cultural adaptability. Regular scenario planning exercises, combined with continuous monitoring of potential trigger events, help maintain readiness for complex cascade scenarios while enabling rapid response when needed.

Building Global Resilience Networks

Global resilience networks have emerged as crucial infrastructures for managing contemporary challenges, connecting diverse stakeholders across geographical and institutional boundaries. These networks serve as dynamic systems that enable rapid response to crises while fostering long-term collaboration for sustainable solutions.

The Mediterranean Resilience Partnership demonstrates how regional networks can effectively address complex challenges. Bringing together coastal cities, environmental organizations, and maritime industries, this network has successfully developed integrated approaches to climate adaptation, migration management, and economic sustainability.

Cross-border collaboration has proven essential in building effective resilience networks. The Greater Mekong Subregion's disaster response network exemplifies how countries can overcome historical differences to create robust systems for managing shared risks and resources. Regular joint exercises and information sharing have strengthened regional capacity for crisis response.

Urban resilience networks have become particularly significant as cities face increasing environmental and social pressures. The C40 Cities network has pioneered innovative approaches to climate adaptation, sharing best practices and resources across metropolitan areas worldwide. These connections enable rapid dissemination of successful strategies and mutual support during crises.

Financial resilience networks link institutions across global markets, enabling coordinated responses to economic threats. The development of cross-border payment systems and mutual support mechanisms has enhanced the stability of international financial systems while providing backup channels during disruptions.

Scientific research networks contribute crucial knowledge to global resilience efforts. The International Research Network on Climate Adaptation has connected researchers worldwide, accelerating the development and implementation of effective adaptation strategies. These collaborative efforts help bridge the gap between scientific understanding and practical application.

Healthcare resilience networks gained prominence during recent global health challenges. The establishment of regional medical supply chains and shared emergency response capabilities has enhanced preparedness for future health crises. These networks continue to evolve, incorporating lessons learned from recent experiences.

Food security networks connect agricultural producers, distributors, and consumers across regions. The African Food Resilience Network has successfully improved food system stability through innovative partnerships and technology adoption. These connections help communities maintain access to essential resources during disruptions.

Technology sharing networks enable rapid dissemination of innovative solutions to common challenges. The Asia-Pacific Technology Alliance has created effective mechanisms for transferring sustainable technologies across borders, accelerating adoption of resilient infrastructure solutions.

Indigenous knowledge networks contribute valuable perspectives on sustainable resource management and adaptation strategies. The Arctic Resilience Network incorporates traditional ecological knowledge into modern resilience planning, creating more effective and culturally appropriate solutions.

Educational networks support capacity building for resilience across communities. The Pacific Resilience Partnership's training programs have enhanced local capabilities while fostering regional cooperation. These educational connections create lasting relationships that strengthen response capabilities.

Infrastructure resilience networks coordinate maintenance and upgrade efforts across regions. The European Critical Infrastructure Protection Network has developed effective approaches to managing interdependent systems while sharing resources and expertise during emergencies.

Water management networks address critical challenges in resource sharing and conservation. The Nile Basin Initiative demonstrates how competing interests can collaborate to ensure sustainable water access while building shared capacity for drought response.

Energy resilience networks support transition to sustainable systems while maintaining reliable service. The Caribbean Sustainable Energy Alliance has successfully implemented regional approaches to energy security, combining renewable resources with traditional systems.

Transportation networks increasingly focus on resilience through redundancy and flexibility. The North American Transportation Alliance has developed effective protocols for maintaining essential connections during disruptions while supporting long-term system adaptation.

Cultural heritage networks protect valuable resources while supporting community resilience. The Mediterranean Heritage Network has created successful programs for preserving historical sites while adapting to environmental changes and social pressures.

Emergency response networks provide crucial support during crises. The Pacific Disaster Center's network connects first responders across regions, enabling rapid deployment of resources and expertise where needed most. These connections have repeatedly proven their value during natural disasters.

Business resilience networks support economic stability through shared resources and expertise. The ASEAN Business Resilience Network has helped small and medium enterprises develop effective adaptation strategies while maintaining regional economic connections.

Future resilience networks will require greater integration across sectors and scales. Success depends on building flexible, adaptive systems that can respond to emerging challenges while maintaining essential functions. These networks must balance immediate response capabilities with long-term sustainability goals.

The continued evolution of global resilience networks represents a crucial adaptation to contemporary challenges. By connecting diverse stakeholders and resources across traditional boundaries, these networks enhance our collective capacity to manage current and future challenges while building sustainable solutions for coming generations.

The Role of Non State Actors

Non-state actors have fundamentally transformed the landscape of global governance and crisis management, wielding increasing influence in shaping international responses to complex challenges. From multinational corporations to grassroots movements, these entities have become essential partners in addressing contemporary global issues.

International NGOs demonstrate remarkable agility in responding to humanitarian crises, often reaching affected populations before traditional state mechanisms activate. During the 2020 Beirut port explosion, organizations like Médecins Sans Frontières provided crucial immediate assistance while coordinating with local civil society groups, showcasing the vital role of non-state actors in emergency response.

Private foundations have emerged as powerful catalysts for global change, deploying significant resources to address challenges beyond the reach of traditional state actors. The Gates Foundation's work in global health exemplifies how private philanthropy can accelerate progress on critical issues through targeted interventions and partnership building.

Civil society organizations increasingly shape policy decisions through advocacy and direct action. Environmental groups have successfully influenced international climate negotiations, while human rights organizations have transformed how governments approach conflict resolution and humanitarian assistance.

Religious institutions continue to play vital roles in community resilience and crisis response. Faith-based networks often provide crucial support systems during disasters, leveraging their deep community connections and established trust to deliver aid effectively and mobilize resources rapidly.

Indigenous peoples' organizations have become increasingly influential in environmental protection and sustainable resource management. Their traditional knowledge and stewardship practices often provide valuable insights for addressing contemporary challenges, particularly in climate adaptation and biodiversity conservation.

Professional associations serve as essential knowledge brokers, facilitating information exchange and standard-setting across borders. Organizations like the International Association of Emergency Managers help establish best practices and coordinate responses to complex crises.

Think tanks contribute significantly to policy development and crisis analysis, providing crucial research and recommendations that inform decision-making at multiple levels. Their work often bridges the gap between academic research and practical application in crisis management.

Social movements have demonstrated remarkable ability to mobilize global support and influence policy changes. Youth climate movements have successfully pressured governments and corporations to adopt more ambitious environmental policies, showcasing the power of coordinated non-state action.

Business networks increasingly engage in crisis response and resilience building, recognizing that their long-term success depends on stable, sustainable communities. Industry coalitions often develop innovative solutions to complex challenges while supporting broader community resilience efforts.

Academic institutions forge crucial international partnerships that enhance global knowledge sharing and capacity building. University networks frequently lead research initiatives addressing pressing global challenges while training future leaders in crisis management.

Media organizations play vital roles in crisis communication and public awareness, though their influence has evolved with the rise of social media platforms. Independent journalism remains crucial for maintaining transparency and accountability in crisis response efforts.

Humanitarian organizations have developed sophisticated capabilities for rapid response and sustained support in crisis situations. Their expertise often complements state resources while providing crucial independent perspectives on complex emergencies.

Technology companies have become influential actors in crisis response, providing crucial infrastructure and innovative solutions for emergency management. Their platforms often serve as essential communication channels during crises while supporting coordination efforts.

Diaspora communities increasingly function as important bridges between societies, facilitating cultural understanding and resource mobilization during crises. Their networks often provide crucial support channels for affected communities while influencing international responses.

Labor unions contribute to social resilience through advocacy for worker protection and sustainable economic development. Their international networks often provide important channels for solidarity and mutual support during crises.

Cultural institutions help maintain social cohesion and community identity during challenging times. Museums, theaters, and cultural centers often serve as vital gathering spaces for community healing and dialogue in post-crisis situations.

Youth organizations demonstrate remarkable capacity for innovation and mobilization in addressing global challenges. Their energy and technological fluency often drive creative solutions to complex problems while building future leadership capacity.

Women's organizations play crucial roles in community resilience and peace-building efforts. Their networks frequently provide essential support services while advocating for inclusive approaches to crisis management and recovery.

The future effectiveness of non-state actors depends on their ability to build legitimate influence while maintaining independence and credibility. Success requires balancing cooperation with various stakeholders while preserving the unique perspectives and capabilities that make these organizations valuable partners in addressing global challenges.

As traditional governance systems struggle with increasingly complex global challenges, non-state actors will continue to grow in importance. Their ability to operate across borders, build trust with local communities, and develop innovative solutions makes them indispensable partners in building more resilient global systems.

www.ingramcontent.com/pod-product-compliance
Lightning Source LLC
Chambersburg PA
CBHW071329130726
47996CB00002B/684